PEGGLES AND PRIMROSES

GW00497159

Overleaf: *The author with her mother and older sister Ruth, 1915.*

PEGGLES AND PRIMROSES

A country childhood

by

NAN COLLECOTT

TERENCE DALTON LIMITED
LAVENHAM   .   SUFFOLK
1989

Published by
TERENCE DALTON LIMITED

ISBN 0 86138 066 5

Text photoset in 10/11pt Century Schoolbook

Printed in Great Britain at The Lavenham Press Limited,
Lavenham, Suffolk

Contents

Chapter One	Matching Tye	1
Chapter Two	Home and Garden	7
Chapter Three	The Shop	13
Chapter Four	Ponds and Ditches	17
Chapter Five	Going to School	21
Chapter Six	On the Farm	27
Chapter Seven	Suffolk Grandparents	33
Chapter Eight	More Suffolk Friends	39
Chapter Nine	Banished to Polstead	47
Chapter Ten	Goings on in Matching	51
Chapter Eleven	Village Church	55
Chapter Twelve	Chapel Affairs	59
Chapter Thirteen	Doctors and the District Nurse ...	65
Chapter Fourteen	Village Blacksmith and Local Farms	69
Chapter Fifteen	Country Walks and the Point-to-Point	75
Chapter Sixteen	London Grandparents	79
Chapter Seventeen	Echoes of India...	85
Chapter Eighteen	Train to School	89
Chapter Nineteen	A New and Exciting World	95
Chapter Twenty	Last Summer at Home	101
Chapter Twenty-one	Cambridge Terms	107
Chapter Twenty-two	Farewell to Cambridge	113
Chapter Twenty-three	The Next Stage	117
Index	123

To my daughter Diana,
without whose encouragement
this would never have been
written.

Acknowledgements

Even when writing a book of personal reminiscences an author finds herself indebted to many people for help and encouragement, and this author is no exception. In particular she would like to express her gratitude to the following for their kind permission to use their pictures as illustrations:

Elsa Totman, of Hixham Hall, Albury, for her sketches; Leonard Little, of Hillingdon Lodge, Harlow, for the photograph of his family; John and Judith Tinney for the photograph of their home, Matching Hall; Patricia Butler, of Stoke-by-Nayland Post Office, for the postcard of Stoke-by-Nayland Church; E. T. W. Dennis and Sons Limited, Scarborough, for photographs of St John's College, Cambridge; and Jarrold and Sons Limited, Norwich, for illustrations from their colour publications of Cambridge colleges.

CHAPTER ONE

Matching Tye

A DOZEN or more cottages still border Matching Tye. This is a small hamlet, part of the scattered village of Matching in Essex. A country road winds up to it from Old Harlow, tarmacadamed over the gravel now. There are still arable fields on either side and a cluster of cottages at the top of Moor Hall Hill.

Moor Hall itself is no more. Mr Balfour, a tall distinguished-looking old man, lived there in an imposing mansion overlooking a lake, and we spent our Sunday School treats in his gardens. On one other splendid occasion he invited the famous Co-Optimists to give a concert there. We country folk thought this the height of sophisticated entertainment. Now the house is demolished, the gardens abandoned and the woods scarred and overgrown.

As you reach the Tye our house is still there on the right, behind a tall hedge, backing up close for shelter under Matching Wood. Kate and Walter Salmon, my parents, settled here in 1910. My only sister Ruth and I were born there; she was two and a half and I was one year old when the First World War broke out. It was my home until I married in 1939, a few weeks before the start of the Second World War.

Memory plays tricks with me. I recall such clear details of most of my childhood in Matching between the two world wars; but those four years during the Great War are only faintly sketched. A spotlight focuses on unimportant, almost trivial, scenes, on a moment of behaviour, on smells and colours. People hardly existed for me, and the only feelings I remember are of happiness and security with my sister and mother.

My father, having previously been a regular soldier with the Royal Horse Artillery in India, was immediately recalled in 1914 and offered a commission. Mother persuaded him to refuse this, because, perhaps mistakenly, she felt he would be subjected to greater risks. Also, there was no doubt that as a retired Regimental Sergeant Major he would be better paid than as a junior officer, and he was already forty-three. He spent all the four war years at the front in France, writing something to my mother every day and posting the letters when he could.

Nancie, seated on the right, and her sister Ruth
with their mother, 1917.

1

Father, in his
Royal Horse
Artillery
uniform.

My mother, tiny and pretty but tough and determined, was left
to cope with us in this lonely house with meadows on each side. I
don't remember any turmoil, impatience or tears; but she must
often have felt deeply unhappy. She loved company and must
have found the loneliness and responsibility a great burden. She
was thirty-six. She worried about my father incessantly.

She was not worried only about his safety: all her life she
worried about his immortal soul. She confided to me much later
that she was always bothered that he might be killed without

repenting. Repentance, apparently, had to be seen to take place. This was part of her strict nonconformist upbringing by her impossible mother, who tackled everyone about the state of his soul, and was the most embarrassing woman I have ever met. Father avoided her always and was obstinately inarticulate about religion. It was such "bad form". I'm sure Mother prayed constantly for him; he would have been so irritated if he had guessed.

My first memory of him is in a blue woollen Red Cross suit and a red tie, deposited at the front gate on his return from hospital at the end of the war. He walked slowly up the garden path leaning on a stick, a tall handsome man, for whom I recall no feelings then at all; he was a stranger.

Yet I remember flashes of life with mother during the war. I have photographs of her with Ruth and me, taken at regular intervals to send to my father at the Front; Mother slim and neatly dressed, with a plait of chestnut hair round the crown of her head; my sister with long hair, usually straight, but curled up in rags overnight and now waving on to her shoulders with white ribbon bows on each side of her head; me, a stolid baby, with thin fair hair reluctant to grow, and starched white frilled knickers inevitably too long for my frock. I'm usually standing on a chair; I probably demanded to be put there.

I can remember a succession of white embroidered cotton frocks with knickers and caps, adorned with pink ribbons to match. Old Mrs Crabbe, the roadmender's wife, commented on them many years later. Mother made all our clothes and we were always dressed alike until we rebelled when we were almost teenagers.

During the War Ruth and I must have had our cots in Mother's room. I remember waking up in the night to find her gone. We screamed in terror. She came hurriedly back; a collection of villagers had gathered at the gate and were strolling along the road alarmed by the red glow in the distant sky. A Zeppelin had been brought down in flames at Potters Bar. The year was 1916.

Having been through the Second World War with my own babies, I marvel at how little the war impinged on us in the country then. There was no fear for our safety, no shortage of food, and I was too young to notice the gaps in the menfolk. So many women were illiterate that Mother often read to them their letters from men at the Front, and wrote the answers. Mrs Crabbe had no children of her own, but fostered three boys who were old enough to be conscripted. She would arrive regularly with a letter in the pocket of her long white apron for mother to read and would add a cross to the letter Mother wrote in reply.

Matching Vicarage was a haven for Mother during the war, particularly at Christmas time and holidays, when she missed my father most. The Reverend J. B. Brinkworth was vicar, a gentle softly-spoken man, short and bald-headed; with a daughter of twelve and a tall outspoken wife. I knew them all well when I grew up, but I remember him only as important then. Every Christmas they gave a party when we played games in the kitchen and had tea in the drawing room. He distributed presents dressed as the Wife of Father Christmas, much less difficult to dress in wartime than a red-cloaked Father Christmas. Ruth and I were quite satisfied.

I must have been an insistent pest. I can see him often sitting at the piano, singing to me:

> Dear little jammy-face,
> How I love you so.
> I wish you were my sweetheart,
> Or my Mam-my.

I demanded it again and again. I still recall the tune. I remember, too, being sent to say "Goodbye" to him; I always announced, "Us am going home!" and he pantomimed floods of tears, whereupon I repeated it again and again in order to evoke such signs of distress. He used the same words to me as an old man when he was leaving after a visit to my home. He was in the background through all my growing up, letting me play with his address stamp in his study, laughing at me when I mimicked people, writing to congratulate me on school successes and giving me college references; finally he would have taken my marriage service in 1939, but he was then too ill.

During the Second World War, he and his wife, having retired to Woodford Green, returned to Matching to stay with my parents in order to escape the Doodlebugs. I joined them from Buckhurst Hill each evening with my first baby to spend the night in peace. Sometimes even there we were under an alert, and he reluctantly came downstairs to please my mother. He confided in me that he felt no fear; the only thing which terrified him was malice and hatred among people he knew. He shrivelled when voices were strident or angry. A very gentle man.

Life in the country was primitive at the beginning of the century. We had no bathroom, no indoor plumbing, no gas, but a privy in the garden, candles and paraffin lamps. The greatest deprivation was the lack of water. There was no piped water in the village, only a pump on the corner of the Tye.

I clearly remember hanging on to the handle of the pail when Mother walked down the road night and morning to fill it at the pump, which mercifully was on the corner of the Tye nearest to us. However, the pump died of suffocation when some bored lads poked an assortment of stones down it. Then Mother had to walk

4

St Mary's Church, Matching.

a mile and a half to the village school, which miraculously had its own water supply. Ruth and I dragged along with her.

By the end of the war we all had piped water; but not indoors. Ours came across the orchard from the road and ended in a standpipe and tap in the garden, on the coldest north-east corner of the house, two sides of the house away from the back door. The struggle was on to prevent it freezing.

I remember little else of those years. Smells are evocative; cooking smells in the kitchen, damp clothes in the wash-house, apples stored on the floor of the spare room. Some colours I remember, too; Mother's brown voile dress with small pink and white roses. I thought she was lovely. There was a rag rug made by my Suffolk grandmother in front of the kitchener; its edges were black, but little tongues or red, blue, brown and white speckled it into a gay muddled pattern.

In 1918 I was five and longing for the adventure of school.

5

CHAPTER TWO

Home and Garden

WOODVILLE, as our house was rather grandly called, stood back from the road in a flourishing garden, lovingly tended by my father. It was pebbledashed, double-fronted, with fading cream paint on the windows and an undistinguished porch over the front door. Its exterior was always shabby.

Before our time it had been two small cottages: a boarded kitchen, a scullery with a heavily beamed low ceiling and two bedrooms above with sloping roofs remained. Two front rooms with bedrooms over, built of lath and plaster, had been added, all unfortunately facing north. My bedroom was at the back, down three steps, over the low-ceilinged scullery, with a loft high above reached precariously with a long ladder. It was on the south side, but the wood pressed so close to the house that the sun hardly penetrated.

The wood was full of birdsong. Owls sometimes sat on the window still at night, calling hollowly to their mates, who answered like an echo from the distant thickets. Bats flew in on summer nights, and I cowered under the bedclothes for fear the old wives' tale was true and they would tangle their feet in my hair.

Although in winter the water tap was muffled in straw and sacking, every day my father's early-morning task was to thaw it out with kettles of hot water, slowly heated on rickety Beatrice paraffin stoves. Then followed the filling up of two huge pails of drinking water to stand in the pantry all day.

A sink had been installed in the darkest corner of the scullery on an inside wall, with a sawn-off pipe underneath and no floor drain—but no-one ever complained to the landlord, Mr Frank Jones, of Housham Tye. That might be courting disaster. Father lived on a small army pension, and he was always afraid of the rent being put up. Perhaps the builder forgot to come back. Outside the paintwork steadily deteriorated; nobody said a word. It remained like that till Father died.

To do the washing-up, Mother continued to collect bowls of soft water from an enormous tank outside the back door, heat it in heavy iron saucepans on the kitchener or on shaky oil stoves, and

Woodville, Matching Tye, our home for many years.

7

turn it into a bowl on a table in front of the window. She dug a fork into a slab of Sunlight soap and whisked it in the water to make a lather. There were no such things as soap powders or detergents. Afterwards the dirty water had to be carried to the chicken run and sloshed into a corner. It produced a wonderful bank of nettles.

I remember Mother than as a little trotting figure, constantly off to the tap, the chicken run, the wash-house or the privy, which hid coyly behind the woodshed.

That privy was a disappointment to me. Grandma's in Suffolk had a much more friendly arrangement; a row of three seats of diminishing sizes, and outside you could peer through a wire mesh and see the results. Ours had only one seat, with a pail underneath. Every Saturday morning my father dug a hole in the chicken run and emptied the contents there. Hers had torn-up magazines in it with hilarious advertisements of hour-glass women in tight stays; ours had dull copies of the *Daily Mail*. There was no indoor sanitation at Woodville until it was sold at the end of the nineteen-forties. The council houses fared rather better; they had cesspools at the bottom of the garden, and the tenants had to work a pole up and down at regular intervals to keep the pipes clear.

Bathing was a blissfully cosy affair; a warm weekly event in front of the kitchen fire. We took it in turns in the tin bath laboriously filled with buckets of hot water, heated on the stove, together with one pail of cold rainwater lifted out of the outside tank, with minute wriggling foreign bodies in it. We took these in our stride. The water was so soft that we could work up a good lather in no time.

Afterwards Father, no longer a stranger but a reserved, thoughtful man, read to us in front of the fire from his large basket armchair. My generation of children had few books, and we wept copiously over them. We sniffed our way through *Uncle Tom's Cabin*, the works of Mrs Henry Wood or Louisa M. Alcott, and an odd slim dark-blue book with a gold curly title, *Jersey Boys*; but best of all we loved *The Lamplighter*. Father skipped all the sentimental parts out of acute embarrassment; this meant continual leaps over several pages, and protests from his bewildered listeners.

Mother had a great sense of the fitness of things. No lack of conveniences would persuade her to cut out her attempts at gracious living. We were never allowed to forget that the house was furnished entirely from Maples. The two front rooms were named pretentiously the "drawing room" and "dining room". The latter was used every day as a sitting room, the former only on Sundays and special occasions as it was so draughty. An incongruous brass standard lamp, inlaid corner cupboards and a beautiful grand piano took up most of the space, but two armchairs, a sofa and several upright chairs to match were squeezed in. Mother battled with the draughts with a gold velvet portière, and sat at the piano to finger out *There is a green hill far away*, her sole repertoire. Visitors were invited to play, and from the age of six I took lessons and practised every day.

Every Monday morning Mother withdrew to the wash-house. She worked as hard as any labourer's wife. Bath loads of dirty clothes stood on a bench. Father had lit the copper early in the morning and steam escaped from the round wooden lid, filling every corner with a warm clean smell and condensing on our bicycles, which leaned against the opposite wall, so that we fought a constant battle with rusty rims. She pummelled and rubbed the clothes in a tin bath, poking those to be boiled into the copper, then lifting them out with a wooden stick and rinsing them in another bath, finally putting them through an ancient clanging wringer.

Two hours later she emerged with an enormous linen basket full of clean clothes and proceeded to fill lines strung round two sides of the house, and when possible spread an army of handkerchiefs over the grass. Most of the next two days were occupied with drying it all, folding it, and ironing it with flat-irons warmed in succession on the kitchener and then clamped into a shining metal slipper.

Although she slaved every morning, Mother had firm ideas on her status in the home. In the afternoons she came into her own. Off with aprons and away with scrubbing brushes; after midday dinner she changed into pretty clothes and uncovered her lovely chestnut hair. She sewed, wrote letters, read or visited, or ran her Baby Clinic or Women's Meeting. She never gardened. There was a firm division of labour, and that was Father's province. He had the townsman's lack of enthusiasm for a kitchen garden, but grew soft fruit and masses of flowers.

There was really no need to persuade him to grow vegetables; all the cottagers grew more than they could eat and were glad to sell them cheaply. Horseradish and rhubarb were in a special category and grew in odd corners. Soft fruit grew in plenty; gooseberries, red and black currants, raspberries and logan-berries. All through the summer they were draped hideously in torn lace curtains in a valiant effort to discourage the birds.

The orchard provided apples and plums galore on old, gnarled, lichen-covered trees. There were huge Blenheim Oranges we saved until Christmas on newspaper on the spare room floor until they were golden and soft and about to wrinkle; hard brown Russets, and juicy red Ribston Pippins. By the gate was a golden gage tree, the only one I have ever seen with such large luscious

Left: A large rambling rose bush almost covered the porch of our home, Woodville.

Opposite page: The orchard at Woodville, with its array of tulips and daffodils.

fruit, which had to be picked at the precise moment they ripened before the wasps beat us to it.

Round the base of every tree were tulips and daffodils in the spring. Mother was allowed to pick all the flowers she wanted, and she filled the house throughout the seaons. When my parents first came to live in the village, before my sister and I were born, the garden was a wilderness. Undaunted, Mother walked the lanes and filled the house with wild flowers. The rooms were small and half a dozen bowls in each room must have been overwhelming, but I grew up thinking it was absolutely right. To this day, the protests of my own family have not completely weaned me from Mother's exuberant method of flower arrangement.

Better still were the flowers in the wood. Only a path and a stream, widening into a pond, separated the back door from the wood. It was privately owned by our landlord, and the keeper reared pheasants for shooting there. However, the Essex Hunt regularly trampled through it, so we saw no harm in wandering at will. In fact Father made an easy bridge across from the chicken run so that he could collect dry wood. We gathered bluebells and

primroses and pale fragile wood anemones from the grassy edges of the centre path. Wild spotted orchids and cuckoo pints abounded; but even then we were not allowed to pick the orchids rashly because of their rarity.

In late summer, armed with walking sticks and baskets and wearing old clothes, we all went blackberry picking in the wood. It sounds energetic, but the blackberries were so plentiful that it was possible to stand still, hook branches towards you, and fill a basket. The brambles themselves were another matter. Thick, luxuriant strands with cruel thorns, allowed to run wild perhaps for centuries, tore our hands and clothes.

Nobody minded if we stopped picking and sat on a tree stump. It was good to be lazy when the wood was filled with birdsong and the sun filtered through the branches.

That wood has been with me all my life. Trees almost touched my bedroom window. Screech owls haunted the nights, cuckoos the spring. All through the summer pigeons called soothingly, and dark shapes of trees are now to me the best part of a winter landscape.

11085

CHAPTER THREE

The Shop

ROADS bounded the grassy triangle which was the Tye on all sides. The pump stood on the apex nearest to us, and across the grass was the only village shop, reached by the road which passed by our house and split the Tye across the middle.

Mr Smith's shop was the village meeting place. It was never a chore to go there on an errand, even when it meant fetching the paraffin in a dirty can held at arm's length to prevent bumping into it. There was sure to be someone there, propping up the counter and gossiping, and there were jars of sweets to be inspected and lots of leaflets to be read at the Post Office end, tied to the wire grille.

Everyone was interested in everyone else, and many of the villagers had nicknames used by us all. Three young men, already out at work, were never known by their real names, but their nicknames were aptly chosen: Whip was thin and supple, Sonny was inarticulate and vulnerable, while Wag was cheerful, with a bantering manner. He caused a constant flutter among the village girls by weaving round the Tye on an incredibly noisy motor-bike.

Our only shop sold most things we needed. Cards of safety-pins, caddies of tea, groceries, ribbons and elastic jostled each other in chaotic confusion on the narrow dark-stained shelves reaching to the ceiling behind the long mahogany counter. The paraffin was fortunately kept apart in a dark, windowless shed leading out of it; but heaven knows what tea-chests and sacks of goods were stored there in the gloom too.

My sister and I spent our tuppence pocket money there every weekend, our choice of sweets invariably regulated by their lasting qualities: a thin rectangle of Sharp's Kreamy Toffee for a penny, liquorice laces, or aniseed balls. We sucked them for hours.

Apart from paraffin and stamps and the odd groceries, Mother bought very little there, because a grocer came round in a van from Sawbridgeworth for orders every week, and as he bought all her surplus eggs, her bill was often cancelled out. Mother kept a very delicate balance between the number of eggs she sold, those she fed us on, and those she pickled in isinglass in an earthenware tub.

Mr Smith's shop on the Tye, with the village pump just visible behind the signpost.

There were often mysterious exchanges, too, of a dozen eggs with another dozen from someone in the cottages. Mother airily explained that we had no cock in the chicken run, but the significance of this escaped us. In due course Father was knocking up coops, Mother mashing up hardboiled eggs, and we were doting on a clucking hen with a brood of yellow chicks.

Mr Smith at the shop was stocky and grey haired. He wore small steel-rimmed glasses which he peered over as they perpetually slid down his nose. Nothing escaped his notice.

The shop looked across the Tye and straight down the Harlow road. Behind the counter he occupied the lookout post; he knew of everyone's movements, and service was conveniently slow so that he could keep an eye on events. He rarely smiled, but he was often jovial in a rather sarcastic way. We feared Mr Smith and found him fascinating; he sucked his teeth. The longer he peered at you while he considered your request, the louder he sucked. He was a deacon at the chapel, and since he sat on the back row, it was impossible to ignore how he punctuated the sermon with his sucking, accelerating as it ended and he rose to take up the collection.

The *Hare and Hounds* public house at Matching Tye.

This was originally two cottages. No longer shabby, the two cottages are now one house. On the left is what was Miss Churchman's cottage.

In the shop he wore a coarse white apron wrapped round him with strings tied in front on top of a rounded stomach. He twisted funnels of rough blue paper in a masterly fashion and scooped sugar and rice and similar dry commodities into them with a shovel. He even tore up sheets of newspaper into squares to twist into cones for sweets; paper bags were almost nonexistent.

His wife was considerably bigger than he was, and also looked down her nose through steel-rimmed spectacles. She was cleverer, too, and managed the intricacies of the Post Office, filling in forms laboriously. Her voice was soft and her laughter quietly amused, as if she had a secret joke.

Two shabby cottages stood at the end of their garden. A labourer lived in one with a family of so many small children that his wife hunted the Bible for names for them; the last one rejoiced in the name of Tamar. The other cottage aimed to rise above its neighbour, and a high dividing fence had been erected. Miss Churchman, a retired governess, had bought it. She found the village in general dull and the people not up to her standard of education; but she was lonely and could rarely pass our gate without wandering in for a chat.

We children were callously amused by her eccentricities. She was certainly short, but she always seemed peculiarly low to the ground; maybe it was her long clothes, which were old and fusty. Everything was topped with a moth-eaten fur necktie. She wore layers of cardigans, a squashed felt hat and dark pince-nez, which were meant to proclaim that she had been in foreign parts. Actually we were fascinated to learn that she had been governess

15

to a Russian aristocratic family before the Great War and had spent much of her working life in St Petersburg.

Her cottage was low ceilinged and beamed, and cluttered with damp books, keepsakes and moth-eaten covers. The cushions were hairy from her mongrel dog, and everywhere had a musty smell. She occasionally asked Ruth and me to tea. We loved to listen to her tales, but she was no cook, so we fed her rock cakes to the dog under the table.

Next door to the *Hare and Hounds* lived the Crabbes. Mr Crabbe, the roadmender, was a round red-faced man in his late sixties, short but powerfully built. He wore a large flat cap outdoors and indoors. Mrs Crabbe always wore an enveloping white apron over a long dark frock with a high neck. She had a rosy wrinkled face and grey hair scraped into a bun on top. She rarely ventured outdoors, but I was often sent on messages to her. The low-ceilinged room was lit by only one window, half obscured by geraniums, and the furniture, lurking in every shadowy corner, was decently covered by mats and antimacassars. The table, with its coarse white cloth permanently laid, stood against the long wall opposite an open-fired range. An odd stale smell pervaded the whole house.

Both old people were kindly. When Mother made her occasional shopping forays to London, Ruth and I were parked on them and we always looked forward to this. Work meant most to them. With no wireless and no television, and since neither of them could read or write, they worked all day and in the evenings too—she at her sewing, he digging in his garden, back still bent. When the light failed outdoors, they sat round the fire for a while, then turned out the paraffin lamp and went to bed under the thatch.

Once a fortnight a large Harrods van swept through the Tye on its way to the Vicarage, calling at half a dozen larger houses. Ruth and I gathered that these people had mysterious things called accounts, but you needed a bank balance to qualify for one. Mother kept us informed about London shops. Apparently The Army and Navy Stores were almost as desirable as Harrods, but neither called at our house.

However, the post brought us endless catalogues from department stores like Barker's, Ponting's and especially Whiteley's, and we spent hours on wet afternoons cutting out paper dolls from them and arranging them all over the kitchen table in family groups. We were even more pleased if the postman also delivered a catalogue from Maples or Waring and Gillows, because we could cut out furniture, too, and put our families in houses.

Very conventional families they were too, with at least two children, and we sent them regularly to church on the kitchen window sill.

CHAPTER FOUR

Ponds and Ditches

WHEREAS in Yorkshire the sound of water is insistent, in East Anglia water is silent, discovered in quiet ponds by the roadside, on village greens, or on farms. Matching had several ponds; the Lily Pond near the church was famous for miles around.

Ours was really only a swollen ditch, separating the garden from the wood; but moorhens lived on our pond. All through the summer moorhens walked delicately on the grass, strutting among the horseradish, clucking rhythmically and flicking their tails.

Their private lives were deplorable. The male had the habit of killing off his mate when she had obligingly laid her eggs, and callously bringing home another mate to the same nest as soon as the first brood had hatched out. He ignored her stiff body floating there, bumping into the bank under the overhanging branches, collecting the scum and elm blossoms. The nest was poised only just above the water, wedged between the branches of a fallen willow tree. The birds made no attempt to hide it; the eggs were visible from the garden and the wood.

This willow tree was a hazard in winter. Skates were too expensive for us, but the moment the ice on the pond would bear us, we were all on, Mother showing us the way to slide. She was expert. During the First World War a fourteen-year-old cousin of hers arrived to help her with my sister and me while Father was away. We were four and five years old. She remembers well how my tiny mother would hurl herself along the slide, part of the pond narrowing into a ditch with a comforting hedge to grab on one side. Then they would drag us along behind them to stop us grizzling with cold on the bank.

When Father returned he insisted on testing the ice before we were allowed on, although he was awkward and it was poor fun for him. He had grown up in Huntingdon and told us of skating expeditions across the Fens to Cambridge.

As we grew older we ventured further afield to the ponds on the farm opposite. This was a dangerous affair. Although the ice bore in the middle, the edges were usually broken and muddy from horses and cattle smashing the ice with their hooves in search of drinking water.

Father and me by the Lily Pond, 1926.

A little further away past the new council houses, with regimented rows of sturdy vegetables filling their front gardens, and round the corner by the gamekeeper's cottage was another pond. This attracted us because it had so much green weed growing on it. We were assured that it was full of fish. It was much too deep for us to slide on the ice there in winter, but in the spring and summer we were frequent visitors. Armed with jamjars, sticks with bent pins on the end of string and bread for bait, we set off with high hopes and spent hours sitting on the bank, dangling the pins in the water.

Very occasionally we landed a tiddler. We popped it into the jamjar of pondwater and carried it home in triumph. Usually our efforts were abortive. It didn't matter. There was plenty of leisure in school holidays.

The Lily Pond was in a hollow among the meadows by the church. A rough road skirted it, and behind it was a spinney of tall fir trees, felled at intervals for telephone poles. We loved to picnic near it. It belonged to Down Hall and had been a private boating lake. The boathouse flanked the road on one side, with a landing stage behind it, but I had never seen a boating party on it; only a derelict boat or two tied up there. A deaf and dumb man, known as Dummy, lived there; we were quite unreasonably afraid of him since he called at our house one night after dark to deliver a

18

message, and we heard him grunt incoherently when Mother called out "Who's there?" as she always did before opening the door in the evening.

Huge flat circular lily leaves floated on the surface of the pond, and among them pale buds and exquisitely beautiful open lily cups in yellow, pink and darker pink stripes, some with smooth and some with jagged petals. Their thick, succulent stems reached to the bottom of the pond, hidden by the leaves, and they multiplied over half the area of the water. People came for miles to wonder over them. Boating would have been impossible. Moorhens walked on the water, picking their way softly across the leaves.

Close by the road was a minute sluice gate through which the water slid from under the lily leaves, tumbled down a few feet, and disappeared under the road. Inside a meadow on the other side of the road was a mysterious shed, only distinguishable from above by a grassy mound, but approached by slippery stone steps descending into the earth to a small dark wooden door. From behind it came a regular thump, like the heartbeat of a resting giant. It filled us with a delicious fear. Once we found the door open and inside, just discernible in the gloom, was a pump—not to be lingered over, because of the louder insistent thumping of its heart. I never understood Father's explanation that water was pumped up from the pond to Down Hall about a mile away.

On the other side of the hill, close by Matching Hall and the church, was another pond. It was our last landmark when we came across the fields to church. Reeds choked it; tall spear-like leaves stood shoulder high, and red hot pokers thrust their dark spikes up taller still. Always some hung broken and trampled where children had tried to pick them; their tough stems defied everything but a sharp knife.

The reeds made an ugly, stiff decoration, but their stems were hollow and we tried to make musical pipes. Some children were clever at producing notes. So they were, too, with new soft shiny holly leaves, which they carefully stripped in the centre, leaving a thin transparent membrane. By holding this to the lips and blowing they could produce a variety of sounds. I could only make an earsplitting sound by blowing with too much fervour.

About a mile and a half away at the other end of our scattered village was a large clear open pond in front of Housham Hall, monopolised by domestic ducks. Magnificent cart horses, lumbering down to drink, disturbed them momentarily, and after dusk when the ducks were safely locked up, the swifts darted in front of the mediaeval barn, diving across the pond, skimming the surface of the water. Years later when the farm became more affluent black and white Muscovy ducks with their red eye-slits were

19

introduced. No need to lock them up; but to keep them safe from foxes an enterprising foreman, known to us all since schooldays as Alfie, indulged his skills to make a house on a raft for them, so that they could settle there at night and be pushed away from the bank out of danger in the middle of the pond.

We could boast no important historical connections in our village, but sometimes we wandered round the edge of the wood and a couple of fields until we reached some meadows where we found the ruins of Oates' barn. We always understood that it referred to Titus Oates, but no one could ever explain the connection with the Plot.

We did know that in the eighteenth century Lady Masham lived at Oates Hall, but this had been burnt down. We knew, too, that John Locke had been a constant visitor; but since we had little idea what a philosopher was, we dismissed this as unimportant. He is buried in the churchyard in the neighbouring village of High Laver. Everyone knew of Lady Masham's ghost: on moonlit nights she rode through the pond in her carriage and pair. I never knew anyone who had seen her.

The meadows attracted us because streams of clear water sang over smooth pebbles and flowed into the pond. We lay on the banks dangling our fingers in the water and collecting bunches of watercress to take home to tea.

Once we found the discarded skin of an adder on the bank; but we saw nothing alive more poisonous than an occasional grass snake sliding through the coarse grass.

The Boat House can still be seen today, virtually hidden by the huge trees.

20

CHAPTER FIVE

Going to School

THE TYE had two pubs on opposite sides of the green, a chapel and, later, a Women's Institute Hall. The village school was a mile and a half away at the junction of a road leading to Newman's End, another Matching hamlet, and a road turning right to the church.

Ruth and I both started at school during the First World War. Like most village schools then, it had only two rooms; a smaller room for infants and a large room for all the other children up to fourteen.

It was dull and dark and the windows were too high for anything outside to cause a distraction; the lavatories were outside and the playground was a bare rectangle of asphalt, devoid of any apparatus for play. I think I always stayed indoors during break; I was small and under age and the boys rushing up and down were rough and clumsy. Mr Gibbins was the headmaster, with one assistant, Miss Nottage, a semi-qualified teacher, to cope with the infants. The schoolhouse adjoined and Mother's friend, Mrs Gibbins, slipped in and out with cups of tea for the teachers. The Gibbinses had two daughters, Maudie and Norah, roughly our ages, whom we knew very well. Perhaps that was why Mr Gibbins let me pull the rope to ring the bell after break and even held my hands sometimes so that I could walk up him when he had relaxed with his biscuit and tea.

All the children had to return home for dinner and come back again for the afternoon. Perhaps I was too tired to rush round the playground. Certainly it was a year or two later that I learned the art of whipping tops, steadying wooden hoops with a stick, playing marbles and skipping.

I can remember painstakingly making rows of pothooks and learning to write. We had slates and squeaky slate pencils for practising at home. I learned my numbers too, but just as I was moved into the big room, Father announced that Ruth and I were to go to Harlow to school. It seemed a very long way away.

It was 1920 and I was seven. Father thought we needed stretching; so every day we walked three miles to Harlow and back. In the summer the return home was a leisurely affair, and we called at several cottages to ask for a cool drink. One white-haired old lady, Mrs Little, who looked rather like a

Mr and Mrs Little and their family, who would supply us with refreshment following our walks.

well-baked cottage loaf, found our demands so persistent that she kept a mug hidden beside the water tap just inside her front gate; we could help ourselves.

Further down the hill, Mrs Farthing lived in the dark little lodge bungalow at the gates of Moor Hall drive. We thought she was a witch. As we went by she was often pottering round her garden, overshadowed by a tall straggling privet hedge. Sometimes she spoke to us; and she confirmed all our worst suspicions by offering to kill the warts on our hands by magic. Sure enough, they eventually disappeared, but probably not because we solemnly spat on them as directed each morning before breaking our fast. When they had vanished she gloated over our hands with her walnut crinkled face and secret grin.

A year later we were doing the journey on our new bicycles. Never a week went by without a puncture; all the roads were gravel. Mr Crabbe, the roadmender, and his mate every morning shouldered their shovels and pickaxes and trudged slowly to work, tickling the edges and filling in the stony puddles. Whenever we passed them we stopped to pass the time of day. Mr Crabbe always had time to lean on his pickaxe and talk to us. He was permanently bowed, and straightened up with some difficulty before he could look at the sky and pronounce on the weather prospects. His speech was slow, his smile gentle; an uncomplaining, inarticulate man.

The nearest Harlow school was Churchgate Street, a church school. No matter: Father was sure I would gain a scholarship in a few years' time. In the meantime a little doctrine and a great deal more discipline wouldn't do us any harm.

The school was built of the same grey stone as the church, and looked an imposing extension to it. I was impressed. The infants' school was a separate building, and the main school had one small room for the seven-year olds and a long, lofty room for every class above that to fourteen year olds.

The headmaster, Mr Webber, took full advantage of this long room. It provided his daily exercise. Twenty times a day he started at one end and for no apparent reason ran as fast as he could to the other end. It was a disconcerting habit until we got used to it.

Churchgate School, Harlow, which so impressed me when I first arrived there. The infants' school is on the left.

Then we watched with interest as he buttoned his jacket, gave a quick tug at his coat tails, and then, legs working rapidly, hurtled past. Rather than slacken speed he leant backwards to apply the brake as he stopped just short of the opposite wall, then twirled neatly on his heels to face back the way he had come. It was a pity there were no hurdles to leap. We dared not laugh.

Mr Webber was a dapper little man, with thinning black curling hair, a finely pointed waxed moustache, and a tense nervous energy. As he spoke to us his eyes flashed, and our attention was riveted on the pulsating muscles of his cheek bones. He must have been gritting his teeth.

His discipline was strict. All our desks were shut or opened together, on command. The noise was deafening, but woe betide the laggard. the offender was interviewed in the cloakroom, propelled there by a mighty shove by the headmaster. Once out of sight among the pegs and outdoor clothes, he seized the culprit by the hair with his left hand, at the same time jerking back his head with his right hand under the chin. Then, breathing hard, with his nose almost touching that of the offender, and face muscles twitching, he leaned over his victim and demanded what he meant by it. It was too awkward a position to maintain, and he was as ludicrous as he was terrifying. It was all show.

I rarely remember him giving corporal punishment, although he flourished a wicked-looking officer's cane at times. Father had a similar one, but it was all part of the game of authority; he never actually used it. Finally Ruth broke Father's up when he had chased her round the garden with it after some particularly exasperating behaviour.

When the headmaster interviewed me in the cloakroom, he always threw back my head by the chin, leaned closely over me and demanded, "What would your father say if he were here now?"

I couldn't tell him that I thought Father would have found the situation highly absurd, so I played into his hands with a meek "I don't know, sir!" which gave him the opportunity to deliver me a little homily. I was his most hopeful pupil at the time, so my behaviour, however innocuous, was always disappointing.

He and his wife were an oddly matched pair. She was taller and fatter, partial to shapeless purple silk knitted jumpers in a holey pattern, and she wore a net to keep her curled fringe in place. Peering over her steel spectacles, she cheered us on to greater neatness in her so-called needlework lessons. I doubt if she was a qualified teacher, but she was a comfortable antidote to her live-wire husband.

Mr Webber's worn-out natural-coloured stockinette combinations were her choicest material. She cut them into small squares

Father, his military bearing in no way diminished by his civilian clothes.

with a hole in the middle and taught us to darn: red wool for the warp, blue for the weft. In this way it was possible to see if we had made a perfectly interlaced darn. I won a prize for this useless accomplishment; everything I've darned since looks cobbled by comparison.

Mrs Webber rarely accompanied her husband on his out-of-school activities. He moved with rapid steps all the time. Topped with a grey Homberg worn at a rakish angle and dressed in a neat grey suit with a gay handkerchief in his breast pocket, he used his walking stick with an extravagant flourish as he hurried to the shops, to the bank or to keep an appointment. Her little fat feet, squeezed into buckled shoes, tottered far too insecurely for her to keep up with him.

In order to stretch his army pension, Father became the School Attendance Officer, covering a wide rural area on his bicycle. He rode at a slow, steady pace, clad in Bedford riding breeches and highly polished gaiters, a trilby hat on his head. When he came to our school I thought how handsome he looked as he leaned nonchalantly on the headmaster's desk, collecting his list of absentees and acknowledging me with a wink. Continued absence or truancy meant a court case for him; he hated these. Even more

25

he hated having to escort mentally defective children on the train to the Peckover Schools at Colchester. It was a far cry from the regiment in India and polo in the sun, but it was preferable to the wastes of Flanders and the Somme. There was always his garden in the evenings.

There were two other teachers in the schoolroom. One was a weedy youth, spotty and earnest, who attached himself to a pretty girl in Standard VII with long fair wavy hair. We thought her outstanding, too. She lived in our direction at Matching Green, a couple of miles further on. In the mornings we sometimes cycled to school with her, but we were discreetly invisible in the evenings when he escorted her home. Eventually they married, so our tact was rewarded.

The other teacher was a young woman with a warm charm, chestnut hair, and an hour-glass figure. She spent five minutes before lessons and during mid-morning break preening herself in the glass doors of the book cupboard and combing out her hair. This operation we watched with fascination. She unrolled the puffs on her forehead in turn, combed them straight out in front of her, then, holding the strand extended, she back-combed it until it disappeared in a soft roll secured by a hairpin. There were three of them to fix.

I can only remember Miss Coleman teaching me my tables and the catechism, chanted in unison. For many years I thought "then" was a verb, because we learned parrot fashion to ask the question: "What did your godmothers and godfathers *then* for you?"

By some odd miscalculation or unwarranted optimism I was sent off to Herts and Essex High School at Bishop's Stortford to take the scholarship examination before I was ten. To my intense embarrassment I was called from the dining room during lunch to be interviewed by a member of staff about this. I wasn't a name—only a four-figure number. It was agony to confess to it in a room full of chatty, confident girls. Had I put the wrong age on my paper? She smiled encouragingly on me. But the paper must have revealed my appalling ignorance; I was not offered a place.

A year later, however, Mr Webber's efforts were rewarded. Letter in hand, he was able to run at full speed down the room, fling open the connecting door between the two rooms, clap his hands briskly, and announce success. I was somewhat daunted because he promptly turned to a photograph on the wall of a woman in a cap and gown, a past pupil of the school, Phyllis Baird, and urged me to be a credit to the school as she had been some years before.

She wore spectacles, had straight black hair and looked remarkably plain. The prospect was not inspiring.

CHAPTER SIX

On the Farm

SUMMER and autumn days were never long enough when we were children. All the year through our leisure pursuits were decided by the seasonal activities on the farm opposite. If we could not join in, we could at least watch. There were six children there, most of them older than us; only Evelyn, the youngest girl, was our constant companion.

When the barns were empty of all but a few bundles of straw or hay, piled high round the sides, we occupied them entirely, arriving with brooms, pans and shovels and playing our endless game of "families". We ignored the festoons of cobwebs looped from the rafters, but swept up the dust on the floor until we were filthy, marked out rooms, improvised utensils and furniture, and sometimes hobbled around in high-heeled shoes and hindered by trailing skirts.

The game was unending. Every evening, every weekend, we carried on where we had left off.

When the barns were full we occupied the waggons and carts in their sheds near the stackyard. These sheds were fortunately intercommunicating through a trapdoor high up in the wall. We felt it was daring to use a ladder to climb through from one shed to another, visiting each other's "houses". You were richer if you were living in a waggon.

Not that we scorned the usual children's games. We trundled our large wooden hoops round the village, hitting and steadying them with a stick; we owned tops of all shapes and sizes, and patterned them with coloured chalks bought from the village shop before we whipped them along the road; and we were skilled with balls and skipping ropes of all lengths, accelerating to the loudly chanted, "Salt, mustard, vinegar, pepper!" We generally reserved these games for the school playground.

As soon as haymaking began we abandoned our games. The warm, sweet smell of new-mown hay drenched the air as the horse-drawn machine cut the grass in swathes and left it lying in flat rows across the fields. Purple and yellow vetches, clover and ox-eye daises threaded through it, dying in the sun. If the weather remained dry the wide rake soon rattled along the road, pulled by a stolid Suffolk Punch, bumping its driver unmercifully as he sat on a sack laid over the projecting metal seat above the prongs. It

Shetlocks Farm, Matching Tye, from which we would collect a jug of milk every day for tuppence.

turned into the field and across the hay, dragging it into fat ragged rows with stubble gaps in between. We knew every process; and since the rake had lived in one of our sheds, we had often tested it and realised how cripplingly uncomfortable the open-work metal seat was.

Now we watched the man regularly lifting the rake and releasing the hay. Afterwards, men with pitchforks turned and tossed it and piled it into small ricks ready for the cart to collect it for the stackyard. Encouraged by the smell and the promise of summer, families carried tea to their menfolk in the hayfield and stayed to picnic with them. We tagged along too, jumping and sliding into the hay, waiting to help fill the cart and escort it back to Shetlocks Farm.

Even more exciting was the beginning of harvest. It fortunately coincided with the long school holidays, and we could spend all day until dusk in the fields or joining in the "carting".

We watched the horse pulling the binder round and round the field. The rotating arms captured the corn as the long blade cut it close to the ground; then the shifting platform underneath shuffled the corn backwards into a bundle, and the tied-up sheaves were spewed out at the back in long rows. We thought the binder the height of sophisticated machinery. Men followed behind to stand the sheaves up in stooks of three or four to dry thoroughly.

Usually it was evening when the last few square yards in the centre of the field were to be cut. Village men and youths gathered with sharpened sticks cut from the hedgerows. The hunt was on. They formed an ever-diminishing circle, watching intently. If they were lucky, frightened rabbits and hares would suddenly flee in all directions. With shouts and flailing sticks, and sharp sickening cries, the kill was made. It was soon over. A few more homes were assured of their supper.

When the sheaves were being carried back to the farm we were almost too busy to return home for meals regularly. We rode out in the empty waggon or cart from the farm, sitting on the "ladders" projecting over the horse's back, if the driver was indulgent. Usually a driver liked company, particularly if they were clearing a field some distance away. Most of the men were good tempered, slow of speech and slow of movement, and quietly amused at our irrespressible energy. Wilfred, the gamekeeper's son, was the youngest driver and therefore our favourite. He had sandy hair, stooped badly, and wore a large flat cap plastered to the side of his head at an angle to match his stoop; he winked at Ruth and gave her a hand to climb in by the big wheels.

Not one of the labourers stripped off his shirt in the hottest weather; it was considered a concession to be allowed to take off jackets. Most of them sweltered in long-sleeved shirts, rolled up over the elbow with a suit waistcoat on top, hanging loose but decently covering their braces.

When we arrived in the field the men got to work with pitchforks passing up the sheaves. We did not wait for the waggon to be filled but attached ourselves to the waiting loaded cart, this time walking with the driver, who usually led the horse home. It was a tiring business.

In the stackyard two men waited by the elevator, tossing the sheaves into the bottom as fast as the elevator could pick them up. The rattling elevator carried them to the top of the stack, where two men pitchforked them into place as they tumbled off. It was a skilled job; the men quickly placed them correctly at the edges to make a neatly rounded stack, ready to be thatched. A stackyard filled with regularly spaced thatched stacks was a most pleasing sight; much more satisfying than stacks covered with untidy sheets of plastic, flapping in the wind, and insecurely held down with old bricks.

Our concern was for the chestnut horse pacing its eternal

circular track to keep the elevator moving. Now and then it was allowed a break, and a drink of water; but all too soon, head down, wearing blinkers, it was patiently striding round again.

In the cool of the evening when the harvest field had been emptied of sheaves, mother sometimes took us gleaning for a few handfuls of corn ears for the chickens. Father never came; he was too proud. Mother understood country ways: she was a farmer's daughter. Father came from the town: the fields belonged to someone else, and he minded his own business.

During the autumn the threshing machine arrived in the stackyard, attended by strangers to the village. This was just one stop in a far-flung itinerary. It had come to wreck the stackyard and demolish the neat stacks, separating the grains of corn from the straw, which was then reduced to chaff. The huge machine was stationary, a dusty aggressive monster powered by a shining steam engine.

The driver lovingly wiped its brass bands with his oily rag, then slowly wiped his hands on it, too, as he surveyed the confusion below him and waited for the sacks to be fitted to the chutes on the side of the machine. Satisfied, he pulled the levers, and the monster roared into life, shuddering as it shook the grain out of its entrails, filling the air with fine dust and escaping chaff.

Ruth and I stood at a safe distance, for fear of being sucked into its bowels, but from our hair to our feet we became permeated with dust.

Men shouted above the hammering noise, sacks were wrenched off and tied up with coarse string, and empty ones hooked on in their place. The full sacks were ready to be despatched by waggon to the local flour mill. We never missed a visit from the threshing machine.

Before the end of autumn the steam engines for ploughing arrived in pairs. They were itinerant, too. One of them pulled a plain shed-like caravan, a temporary home for the men working the engines; it was dumped on some suitable grass verge beside the road. The other pulled the great reversible plough. We wandered the fields to watch these ploughs at work. The two giants took up positions opposite each other across a field, linked together by a massive steel cable. The plough travelled backwards and forwards as each engine throbbed in turn, pulling the cable round the drum beneath its belly, winding and unwinding like twin typewriter ribbons. The furrows were deep and dark. Flocks of seabirds wheeled and swooped over them, searching for food in the newly-turned soil. Rough weather on the coast had driven them inland.

We were fascinated; but the fear I have of big machines must date from those days. Steamrollers mended our gravel-laid country roads. We had to pass them on our way to school in Harlow, and I hated cycling past. David Anderson, a farmer's son with whom we were at school, was cycling past a steamroller on his way to school one morning when his front wheel caught in a rut and he was thrown in front of the roller. No-one could stop it in time; he was crushed to death. I remember David's solid, serious appearance, and his tragic death, and not much else about him.

Another tragedy in Matching made an indelible mark, too. One of the village boys was out with the older men on his first shooting party when he foolishly climbed a stile with his gun loaded. He tripped and fatally shot himself. Horror spread through the village as details were recounted. Even the doctor who gave him morphine was shattered.

I shut my mind to the details. He had been a quiet, handsome boy.

CHAPTER SEVEN

Suffolk Grandparents

MOTHER'S sunshade was a delight; its use marked a special occasion. Nondescript underneath, it wore a white detachable cover in Indian muslin, with a stiffly starched frill around the edge. It was a relic of more spacious days in India, and Mother was in the mood to be a lady when she slowly opened it and tilted it over her shoulder.

The first time I remember it as a pièce-de-résistance was during the First World War, when on a summer's day a horse-drawn charabanc was hired to take the villagers for a day's excursion to The Retreat at Theydon Bois, near Epping and Loughton.

The charabanc was full. Ruth and I climbed to the open top deck and sat so near the trees that we could touch them. Mother sat between us, dappled in the sun by the frill of her sunshade.

For years that long, straight undulating road dogged my memory. Travel by car never revealed the same vista. Not so long ago I travelled from Epping to Woodford on a double-decker bus, and once again in my imagination I was three, in starched white cotton, under a lovely sunshade, jogging along behind a pair of black horses.

Every year we spent a fortnight with Mother's parents in Stoke-by-Nayland, just over the border in Suffolk; and, since Matching was three miles from Harlow station, summer holidays always began with a drive in a horse-drawn cab. The black, polished cab drew up grandly at the front gate. Ruth and I had been ready for hours. The cab swayed dangerously as we climbed up on the swinging step and sat facing each other on navy-blue upholstered seats. Its smell and its elegance delighted us. A man in a top hat, clutching a whip, closed the door behind us, and we peered excitedly out of the windows. He climbed up in front, high above the horse's back, exposed to hot dust or rain, and as he shook the reins the black horse stepped smartly out. It was stuffy inside, and we rocked gently as we covered the gravel road, grass verges slipping quickly by on each side.

Father never came to Suffolk. He made the excuse that the chickens needed looking after, or the kitchen required redecorating; really he found it difficult to fit in with Mother's relations.

Grandma Fletcher outside her cottage on top of the Downs at Stoke-by-Nayland.

33

They were simple tenant farmers, narrowly religious, and they spoke with the sing-song Suffolk lilt. He loved a simple life too, but his parents had been comfortably off, town bred, and he was well educated. Any mention of God and religion was horribly embarrassing to him; Grandma Fletcher, never one to miss an opportunity of saving a soul, launched into an intimate examination of both at the drop of a hat.

Even as a young child I hated to be left alone with her. She so obviously thought I needed saving and that it was her duty to put me on the right path; she steamrollered over my feeble protests that I loved Jesus with a firm, "Oh no, you don't!" I had an unfortunate habit of bringing this on myself by bursting out singing, without thinking, the chorus, "I love Jesus, He's my Saviour . . ."

It was discouraging: I was brought up to take Sunday School lessons very seriously, and I had been well grounded in Bible stories and evangelical choruses. In fact I was a particularly pious child and felt that Jesus was very close to me, walking beside me and helping me with all my everyday problems, particularly, as I grew older, examinations. I cut Him very much down to my size, and I was almost grown up before I really appreciated that God was not as small-minded as I was, and that He was not going to punish me every time I cut out church on Sundays. Even when I was eighteen and at college in Cambridge, I sometimes felt driven to come back from a picnic on the river on Sunday to go to Evensong at St John's College Chapel, half expecting a thunderstorm to fall on me if I didn't. I must have surprised and bored my more worldly friends.

Mother was the youngest but one of five children; all the others were boys. By the time she was grown up her parents were old. Grandpa had retired by the time I knew him, and they lived on the end of a row of little white plastered cottages on top of the Downs at Stoke-by-Nayland.

Grandpa Fletcher, tall, broad-shouldered and ruddy, dressed in thick hand-sewn suits, spent much of his time reading his Bible in a shabby, red-leather high-backed chair in the cottage doorway. He was quiet and amiable, not bothered about our souls, and a foil to his good-hearted but sharply-spoken wife, who for all her tiny size was a terror to us all. With a fuzzy white fringe beard edging his chin from ear to ear and his benevolent smile, he was to Ruth and me in the same category as Father Christmas.

Soon after our arrival he picked up a large basket and a roughly-made walking stick and put on a roomy trilby hat. We followed him into the pine wood behind the cottage. It was quiet there. Pine needles were soft to our tread, and the scent was exotic.

Grandpa Fletcher seated in his high-backed leather chair.

Grandma Fletcher, who dressed in her finest clothes for chapel on Sundays.

We were there to work; the basket had to be filled with cones for the fire. There were hundreds lying on the ground; long closed cones; short wide-open cones like gaping teeth; and beautifully-shaped cones, open at the base but closed at the top, resting upright in the palm of your hand, brittle to the touch if you pressed too hard. We burnt them on the open hearth if the evening was cool.

For breakfast there was home-cured bacon. Most country people kept a pig at the bottom of the garden in those days. Grandma disappeared into a small storeroom and returned with slices cut off the joint hanging there on a hook; they were uneven in thickness and an odd brown colour, but the smell was mouth-watering as they spat on the stove, and the special taste was unforgettable.

Grandma's cutlery had black horn handles and sharp three-pronged forks. We were shocked to see that she sometimes ate off her knife. Her plates, painted in muted colours, were criss-crossed with fine cracks, and in some places the earthenware felt rough where the edges were chipped. It was different at home; but Mother never commented. She, too, looked different in her pretty muslin clothes and chestnut hair beside her mother in a long thick black skirt and high-necked black tucked blouse, her thin grey hair scraped back into a tight bun from a centre parting. Grandma used a villainous-looking steel comb to scratch it down more firmly.

She wore tight black-buttoned boots, too. Ruth and I knew,

because she sat between us on top of the Downs, and as we slid down we pulled her with us, each grasping a small black-buttoned foot. She must have been more fun than I remember; I recall her caustic tongue more readily than her amused smile.

Grandfather died quite soon after our first visit and Grandma moved to a white bungalow in Scotland Street. We spent some time there each summer, always a little doubtful of sleeping on the ground floor since a toad jumped through the open window one evening, and we had to persuade it to leap into a paper bag so that we could drop it outside again. Dozens of snails lived in the low box hedges around the front flower beds. We had to collect them in a tin each Sunday morning and take them up the road to feed Aunt Mary-Ann's chickens. It was really a means of occupying us while Mother and Grandma put on their Sunday finery for morning service at the chapel. Regular attendance at chapel was part of the ritual of holidays.

The chapel stood at the end of Aunt Mary-Ann's long market garden. There were peach trees growing along one wall. Small and indomitable, with her hair raked back under a black bonnet tied under her chin and wearing a long black silk dress under a

Lizzie and Charlie Riddlestone's cottage at Stoke-by-Nayland. Lizzie was the village dressmaker.

jet-trimmed cloak, Grandma would settle herself at the end of a row by the centre aisle. She was an authority on the Bible, her sole reading matter, so woe betide any careless preacher.

The congregation was too small to warrant a regular minister, so the pulpit was filled in the mornings by a variety of earnest, but not always articulate, lay-preachers. In the afternoons Mr Sawdy, the minister from the parent chapel in Nayland, took the service. He was lean, with a longish moustache and glasses, and a curious habit of scooping up cake crumbs with his teaspoon if he came to tea on a pastoral visit.

Sometimes the Salvation Army's Boy Scouts were camping over the hill at Valley Farm, and Ruth and I were overjoyed to have them to provide the music for the service. The whole place rocked with the noise of the brass band, and an odd wink from the boys kept us on our toes. Grandma thought they were the work of the Devil. She had the oddest but most steadfast prejudices. Girl Guides, Boy Scouts and aeroplanes were wrong; there was no argument about it. There were no shades of grey in her thinking; we were all going straight to Heaven or to Hell.

She listened intently to the sermon, and to my embarrassment commented aloud if she disagreed. Her back would stiffen with disapproval; I watched nervously for the signs. At the end of the service she lost no time in waylaying the preacher the moment he stepped down from the pulpit. She soon put him on the right path.

It was a great relief when, after I was eleven, it became my holiday task to play the American organ for chapel services. However, the organ was placed directly beneath the pulpit, and a particularly vociferous preacher was inclined to spit on my head.

The congregation liked me to play because, as one old lady, Mrs Peartree from a cottage in Polstead, said to me, "You make the organ talk, my dear—you play with such feeling!"

I blush to recall my sentimental abandonment to pumping and squeezing. At least I was accurate, whereas the village dress-maker, Lizzie Riddlestone, whom I supplanted, was like a grasshopper leaping frenziedly from note to note in a wild attempt to hit the right one. She swayed jerkily backwards and forwards as her feet pumped the bellows and she peered at the music over her steel-rimmed spectacles.

Her husband Charlie sometimes sang solos to her accompaniment. Such loyalty and devotion deserve mention. Regardless of rhythm, tune, or discords he continued to the end; his wife, faint but pursuing, followed on the organ. He had a peculiarly husky voice, always wore a smart grey suit on Sundays, and had a horn of thick white hair brushed up on each side of his head. For all his religious fervour, he had an unexpected sense of humour and a twinkle in his eye.

Emmie Welham on Well Field, Stoke-by-Nayland. There was a path across this field from Scotland Street to Valley Farm.

There were times when Emmie, Aunt Mary-Ann's only daughter, ten years older than I was, felt inspired to give a violin solo—*Il Traumerei* was the favourite—and we practised hard before the service began. These occasions were cosy, because Emmie usually stayed on the organ seat with me throughout the rest of the service, and her wit at the expense of the preacher was, I thought, devastating. I can remember being convulsed with giggles when she took a searching look behind her at the preacher above, who was shuffling his notes written on pieces of card, and whispered fiercely to me, "My goodness me—he's telling our fortunes!"

After the afternoon service it was tradition to walk up the hill to the Angel corner, then turn right for a mile or so down to Polstead to accompany Mrs Peartree back to her cottage. It was time for Mother to have a gossip. Ruth and I were happy to run in front and follow detours to look at the mill or explore the river bank. Every summer we walked miles in Suffolk on roads, tracks and meadows; strange how summers seemed always warm and sunny, time endless and unhurried.

Sundays were highlights in our Suffolk holidays, stimulating and social occasions to punctuate our simple lives. Transport and communications have made possible such a variety of pursuits now; twice-a-day chapel services have been squeezed out.

The chapel has gone; transformed into a desirable house. The peach trees have been cut down.

CHAPTER EIGHT

More Suffolk Friends

A LL through the Twenties Ruth and I looked forward eagerly
to these visits to Suffolk, even though all of Mother's
relations, except Emmie, seemed to us incredibly old. Perhaps
they were just old-fashioned in their dress.

Aunt Lizzie, the wife of Mother's brother Arthur, seemed
always old. Kicking out her long black skirts as she walked
quickly along, she seemed for all the world like a French curé on
parish business; flat black hat covering hair combed up on top of
her head, her tall thin body straight as a ramrod. Like so many of
her contemporaries and all of Mother's older relations, she had
only a few remaining teeth in front, discoloured and uneven like
worn-down groyne posts. She nibbled; they all nibbled. They tore
pieces off tough food by pegging it firmly in their few front teeth;
or they gave up the unequal struggle and dunked it in their tea.

With a smooth gliding motion she was always hurrying along
the road, anxious to reach her destination. She was never known
to wait long for a bus, and if it was late she would set off to walk,
often covering ten or twelve miles even when she was over
seventy.

Her peculiar hats were an unfailing source of furtive amuse-
ment to us children. We made excuses to disappear when we
visited her and she was safely engrossed in conversation so that
we could try them on, prancing in front of a mirror. Not only were
they flat crowned but they were decorated, too, with an odd bow, a
stiff feather or a faded flower. We longed to have them in our
dressing-up box. While we played, Mother was testing Aunt's
home-made wine, cowslip, rhubarb or parsnip. Mother always
protested that all wines went straight to her head, and would
never willingly taste alcohol; but because they were home made
Aunt's wines were acceptable. She sipped and gossiped happily.

Aunt Lizzie had been a nurse in London before her husband
retired and they came to live in Stoke, near my grandmother.
They bought two adjoining cottages, let one and lived in the other.
It was poky, cluttered with furniture and china, and hopelessly
dark and inconvenient. Years later, when she came with my
mother to visit me, she commented with amazement, "What a lot
of windows to keep clean!"

Her husband died quite soon after settling at Stoke. She had one married son, but lived alone. No member of the family could be in trouble without Aunt Lizzie turning up quietly and without fuss, clutching a small case, often having walked miles. She hardly knew my father, but she was there to help my mother when he was dying of cancer. I remember so well her saying quietly, when Mother comforted herself that he was so weak that he would slip away easily, "Yes, but there's always an anguish in dying."

I hoped she was wrong. A few years later she was back again to help my mother, who was crippled with arthritis in her old age: a kind, unobtrusive soul, capable and reassuring—someone to be leaned on.

To us Aunt Mary-Ann was always old, too. She and her husband, Frank Welham, had a smallholding further up the hill in Scotland Street, and lived in a typical pink-washed Suffolk cottage, inappropriately called *The Laurels*. By the gate there certainly was an ugly spotted laurel bush, but the uneven brick

The Laurels, Scotland Street, where Frank and Mary-Ann Welham lived.

path, garden beds and gravel drive had no affinity with the drab villa-type house conjured up by the name. I loved staying there; and my four children, when they were very young, came to love it too. It was there that we first climbed narrow, steep, cottage stairs, leading straight up out of the living room behind a wooden-latched door.

Frank was busy from morning till night, stoking the fires in his greenhouses, hoeing his vegetables or watering his choice plants from a huge oval swinging tank which he pushed up and down the paths. He fitted in odd-job gardening in his spare time, too. Every part of his acre of land had to be productive; there was no sign of a lawn where they could sit in the sun. This was typical of cottage gardens then. No one could afford a lawnmower and any grass had to be cut by hand, orchards with a scythe and ornamental pieces with shears. This was laborious and time-consuming; vegetables were more profitable.

Mary-Ann was a slight figure in a high-necked blouse and a long black skirt, usually covered with a starched apron. Her two remaining front teeth were to the left of centre in the top jaw, so she clamped them over the bottom lip, giving her a questioning, apprehensive, air. She hurried round the cottage with an uncertain gait, as if blown by the wind, stumbling over steps and touching walls as she moved from room to room. A diseased middle-ear had left her deaf and had upset her balance. It also caused her great mental stress, but of this we were only dimly aware.

Behind their friendly three-seater privy there were three outbuildings, including a lofty stable. At the back of this, where it was dark and cobwebby, was a deep well which was for many years their only water supply. After a swift look down into the yawning, menacing hole, apparently bottomless, Ruth and I were too afraid to go near it; but we could see the overhanging pulley and bucket as we peered round the dilapidated door. Emmie, her daughter, told us later that Mary-Ann was once discovered leaning precariously over it, distraught. Her diseased ear and the loneliness provoked by her deafness had led her to contemplate suicide. We knew her only as a quiet, busy figure, kind and remote, constantly dabbing a large white handkerchief to her discharging ear.

Her pantry was the centre of the house. It was long and rather dark, reached by an uneven wooden step. It was her pride and joy, and a treasure house of culinary delights; row above row of jars of home-made pickles, chutneys, marmalade, jams and lemon curd. On wider shelves stood large bottles of pears, plums, peaches and beetroots; and on the floor stone jars of French and runner beans preserved in salt, and earthenware pans of eggs in isinglass. On

41

wide slate shelves, temptingly and conveniently low, was set out the food she cooked from day to day.

As a young woman she had been in service at a large local mansion and her employers had sent her to London to learn the art of cooking at one of the few private cookery schools. She returned to become their head cook. She was an artist with food; it was never too much trouble, even when she was old, to produce subtly flavoured puddings, professionally decorated cakes and smooth, delicious sauces for ordinary weekday occasions. She would serve delicacies in aspic, and apple moulds studded with blanched almonds; or bone and stuff a chicken or turkey for a picnic. She was a very simple woman; but superbly professional.

I once rashly offered to cut up runner beans for lunch. She looked with disappointment at the resulting colander full; much too chunky. I was promptly given a demonstration; each slice must be long and equally thin.

Ruth and I were immensely attracted to Emmie. She was red-haired, passionate, and full of lively ideas. Because she was ten years older than we were we hung on her words and followed her lead. By some odd calculation my grandmother was her Aunt Emily; we never properly understood the relationship, but we did understand the healthy respect she had for our grandmother, who totally disapproved of her gay and wanton behaviour but had a grudging admiration for her defiant spirit. Grandma was cunning. She would say to Emmie, "It was noisy here last night with people passing late down the road. What was on the in the village?"

"A Whist Drive."

"Were you there?" she demanded swiftly, and then rounded fiercely on Emmie for her sinful behaviour. They carried on a constant battle of wits.

When we were older and could be put on the train at Bishop's Stortford and trusted to change trains at Braintree for the Colchester line, we went alone to stay with Aunt Mary-Ann. We were flattered to be invited without Mother, who became a little doubtful of these visits. She had her suspicions that we were being told the facts of life in some detail. She was right; but it saved her the acute embarrassment of tackling the job herself.

Emmie put herself out to entertain us, often at her mother's expense. At table, after breakfast, Mary-Ann insisted on reading a Bible passage aloud from a book of daily readings. Emmie was exasperated by them and maintained that she knew most of them by heart as they'd been through them so many times. From the first words she muttered her protests. Since her mother was so deaf she was oblivious to the ribald running commentary. In any case she had to concentrate hard, because she had to look at each

Valley Farm at Stoke-by-Nayland, overlooking the Stour.

word carefully to be sure she read it correctly. It was cruel—and hilariously funny. We were a most appreciative audience.

Emmie's comments and our reaction to them brought mild protests from her uncomfortable father, who was equally bored but patient, "Now then, stop it altogether. Leave your mother alone."

It had no effect on Emmie, who was well into her stride. Her mother's voice droned monotonously on, slowly emphasising every word, Emmie challenging every statement. We tried to be as insignificant as possible, but we constantly exploded into giggles, of which we had the grace to be mildly ashamed.

Sometimes we were treated instead to an alarming little box full of neatly rolled-up texts. Mary-Ann took a pair of tweezers and extracted a roll. Then she slowly read the text out to us; for her it was a divine message with a particular relevance to the day ahead. Emmie was not convinced, and said so. Ruth and I found it disconcerting, and rather chancy, too.

But the days were filled with adventure; familiar haunts to visit, acquaintances to renew and new places to explore. We roamed over Well Field to Valley Farm, stopping on the way to paddle in the river or to float our grass "boats" under the bridge. Passing the bridge always took time because we had to hang upside down or turn somersaults on the metal bars in their concrete posts. Cows wandered down to drink at the ford in the meadow, but the fast-running water over the pebbles was so clear that we could drink it too.

At the farm we watched for hours the old wooden barrel turning round and churning the cream into butter. It was a poorish farm on stony, unproductive land, not like the fertile Essex soil on the farm opposite us in Matching, where the farmer's wife had a

43

beautiful shining separator and churn. Here in Suffolk Mrs Lord, the farmer's wife, worked hard all day long, trudging round in a sack apron and gumboots. She cheerfully fetched water from the pump, scrubbed brick floors, chopped wood, fed the hens, and patted her yellow butter into half pounds. Ruth and I followed her everywhere.

When she sat down exhausted, I played her old grand piano which was hideously out of tune. She was slim and pretty with curly hair, and on Sundays she dressed in fashionable clothes like my mother, looking very smart when she was in chapel. We never thought of her as old. Grandma admired her hard work on the farm, but scoffed at her foolish desire to be fashionable.

Several years later she was still working just as hard, with no help as she grew older. While chopping sticks she lost the sight of one eye when a piece of wood flew up and hit her in the face, but even that handicap failed to repress her cheerfulness. Until she was an old woman she still walked across the fields to the village, undaunted by the mud and the steep hills; or she climbed the long stony lane out of the valley to Park Road and along to the crossroads to catch an occasional bus to Colchester or Hadleigh. For weeks in the winter the valley was cut off. The only visible habitation was a hill farm in the distance.

To Ruth and me, when we were eleven and twelve, part of the attraction of the farm was the good-looking son, Dick, who was almost too shy to speak to us; and the Boy Scouts who camped there every summer.

Mr Lord was short and slow moving, softly spoken, lazily teasing my pretty sister. During the Second World War the War Agricultural Committee took over their inefficiently farmed land and the Lords moved to a small cottage nearer Polstead. Mr Lord died first and his wife ended her life in a home. All their hard work brought them so little reward.

Often as children when we returned from visiting them we came a long way round over the hills, calling at remote farmhouses if Emmie knew the occupants. It was rumoured that there had been incest between brother and sister at one of these isolated homesteads; it seemed impossible to explain the girl's baby in any other way. It was spoken of in hushed tones; but we were unperturbed, not really understanding the significance of what we heard. They were pleasant, robust young people; the only time we met them was when they had walked miles across the fields to a chapel service.

The river was our favourite picnic site. A bottle of lemonade, a bag of sandwiches and as much fruit as we could stuff into our pockets, and we were free from morning till dusk. Every Suffolk holiday followed the same familiar routine; we never found it dull.

We built dams with sticks and pebbles, or lay on the bank, idly dabbling our fingers in the water. While the others paddled and enjoyed it, I was often a nuisance, as the cold water produced miserable pains in my legs; I often chose to ignore these warnings until I was in tears on the bank with someone massaging my legs fiercely. When we finally consulted our doctor at home, he put it down to "growing pains", and advised me to lie in bed at night with my toes turned up and my heels stretched down. I conscientiously followed his advice with no obvious result. Today I expect it would have been recognised as a form of rheumatism.

The chapel at Scotland Street in which I used to play the organ is now a house.

CHAPTER NINE

Banished to Polstead

O N ONE of our visits to Suffolk Mother had to nurse my sick grandmother at the bungalow. Ruth and I were too young to be useful, so it was arranged that we should stay at a farm in the neighbouring village of Polstead, famous for its cherries, "Polstead Blacks", and for Maria Marten of the Red Barn. We were to stay at Cherry Tree Farm, outside the village.

Polstead always produced a certain *frisson* in us because Emmie had regaled us with the horrific story of Maria Marten's murder in detail. Maria, the daughter of a farm labourer, was seduced by the squire's son, William Corder, who after presenting her with at least one illegitimate baby found she was tediously trying to persuade him to marry her. He was finally driven to plan a pretence elopement with her. Dressed as a man, a suitable disguise for travelling, Maria met him secretly in the Red Barn one night, but instead of taking her to London he murdered her there and buried her body under the barn floor. Having thus disposed of the evidence, he proceeded to London; corn was subsequently piled on the barn floor.

Mrs Marten was not convinced that her daughter had gone to London with Corder, however, and was the more upset when she failed to return or to communicate with her. Three times she dreamed that her daughter was "under the corn". Finally, to satisfy her, all the corn was shifted out of the Red Barn and the floor was dug up. Maria's murdered body was revealed.

Corder was immediately suspected, but in the meantime he had married in London and had disappeared. Eventually he was found and brought back to Bury St Edmunds, where he was tried at the Assizes. The trial attracted enormous publicity and controversy, and when he was found guilty and was hanged the public rejoiced at his punishment; his body was sufficiently mutilated for some of his skin to be used to bind a book about the trial.

That was Emmie's story. It was a tale, of course, that had become the theme of a popular Victorian melodrama.

When we used to walk past Maria Marten's cottage in a lane on the Stoke side of the village, or past William Corder's lovely black-and-white house closer in, we cast anxious sidelong glances

The house which was occupied by William Corder, the famous Red barn murderer.

47

at the buildings; but we were full of morbid curiosity. Both houses are quite near the road through the village, but fortunately to reach Cherry Tree Farm on the other side of the village we had no need to go through Polstead itself.

Each day Ruth and I set off over the Broom Hills to visit Mother at the bungalow, to reassure ourselves that she was still there. There was, of course, no telephone. Then we walked all the way back again, at least two miles each way. We passed Aunt Lizzie's cottage and then left the road to cross the water meadows where kingcups and merry milkmaids grew in profusion until we reached the footpath leading over the hills.

We quickened our pace here; the hills were lonely and untenanted except for the rabbits. We followed a narrow track into the valley and over the next hill; on all sides of us, as far as the eye could see, the land was covered with thick bushes of yellow broom. This brought us out on the other side of Polstead. We turned into a long rough lane, bordered on both sides with cherry trees, and came to the farm, with its noisy hens and dogs in the yard. The pump stood there, meadows beyond, and cows being milked in tumbledown sheds.

The young tenant farmer and his wife were poor and struggling, but they were kind enough, and we were adaptable so long as we were together. We were free to roam at will. Once when we were helping to drive some cows back from quite a distance I rode on the back of one. Perhaps I was moaning because I was tired. We were amazed that the cow allowed me to sit there as it jogged along; it was not a particularly comfortable seat, but for me it provided a rest from stumbling along in the ruts.

Evenings were sometimes difficult there because although I was willing to play their tinny piano, Ruth hated to perform. She was shy and obstinately refused when they pestered her. We went up to bed to escape them.

For many years Bertha was a familiar tramp in this area. She plodded the roads in high boots, bundled up in oddly-assorted garments, a felt hat tugged on down to her ears. She was always solitary, always doggedly pursuing some set course. Sometimes she felt particularly anti-social and showed her disapproval of any passing traveller who presumed to stare at her by fierce mutterings and by turning her back. Then she would stop by the side of the road and, in impotent defiance, lift her skirts and thrust out her behind. Ruth and I thought she was very rude. Sometimes when she felt the need of company she would arrive on the doorstep of a remote cottage or farmhouse well before breakfast, expecting a meal and often offering in return a pound of sausages she had bought in the nearest town. She was a frequent visitor to Mrs Lord, and never went away empty-handed.

Polstead Church seen from across the park.

Polstead was one of her favourite stopping places because she liked to spend the night in the church porch. Polstead church is set in the middle of a park; clearly she was determined not to be disturbed. She also resented being kept waiting. On Sunday evenings she was known to mutter rudely at members of the congregation leaving church after the service in a too-leisurely manner; she was anxious to settle down for the night.

Tramps were a familiar sight in my childhood, particularly along the main road through Harlow. They trudged the twelve miles between the two workhouses, Haymeads at Bishop's Stortford and St Margaret's at Epping, leaving one after breakfast and reaching the other in time for a night's sleep. We children were a little intimidated by them, chiefly because they were so dirty and so much inclined to talk to themselves; but they were usually oblivious of people. They kept their eyes on the ground and their possessions in a box on wheels, in an old pram, or slung in untidy bundles on their backs. It was hard to believe what was said about some of them, including Bertha, that they preferred the itinerant life to the comforts and responsibilities of a rented house. I suspect it was easier to believe that than to feel in any way responsible for their miserable plight.

49

One route to Haymeads was up Warwick Road in Bishop's Stortford, and since the Girls' High School is near the top of this road there was a great scare in the Twenties when one of the newly-arrived tramps developed smallpox. The health authorities decreed that all of us girls must be vaccinated, and so it was; except for Ruth and me. Mother could be as obstinate as her mother. She remembered that before going to India someone had died after being vaccinated, and she flatly refused to have us vaccinated; and won her case.

Ruth and I hated being different from everyone else.

Every August bank holiday Stoke had a flower show and fair in Tendring Hall park. We loved it. It was the highlight of our holidays. Emmie entered every competition possible, from dressmaking to flower decorations. We watched her elaborate preparations and helped her to gather flowers. She always won several prizes, and we were a gratifyingly appreciative audience. Round and round the marquees we wandered, looking for tickets on her exhibits; we were proud to claim a connection.

The fair in the evening was unforgettable. The steam roundabout just inside the main gate let off a piercing whistle and we scrambled up the moving steps, clinging desperately to the twisted-barley-sugar brass columns and struggling on to the backs of our chosen horses. It had to be a horse; cockerels were stupid. We had to climb on while the roundabout was still slowing down; we could squeeze in an extra turn or two, and anyway it just might not stop for us.

The daring young man who stood on the platform throughout the ride, leaning inwards as the horses gathered speed, walked nonchalantly from horse to horse to collect our fares. It was difficult to hold the moving brass column with pennies clamped in a sticky hand, but one hand had to be free to clasp the reins. More difficult still to let go and pay the fare.

Threepence a ride. We never had money enough for more than a couple of rides, but we scrambled for horses on the outside circle so as to prolong the rides as long as possible. If we dared look, too, we could see over the heads of the people to the stalls beyond; but as we pranced faster and faster colours and lights sped by, and we were conscious only of the excitement and the need to hang on tightly.

It was too warm and smelly on the inner circle; and the tune of *Bye, Bye, Blackbird*, churned out repeatedly by the steam organ, was deafening, although the man with the oily rag who lovingly tended the engine seemed not to notice.

From a distance, even from over the hills of Well Field back at Grandma's bungalow, the tune sounded gay and exciting. We fell asleep still caught up in a colourful world.

CHAPTER TEN

Goings on in Matching

WE HAD village fêtes in Matching too. Every year the grounds of Down Hall were thrown open to raise money for village activities. Mrs Calverley, who lived in this mansion in vast parklands between Matching and Sheering, was quite the most colourful person in Matching, tall, loud-voiced, with a liking for purple and big hats. She made a splendid figure when she rode with the Essex Hunt, mounted side-saddle, with a veil to tie on her top hat and a bunch of Parma violets in her buttonhole. She brought a presence to all local occasions, and enjoyed playing hostess for these fêtes, which took place every July. They were heavily insured against rain, which perversely fell most heavily in this month.

Everyone walked or cycled to the fête. From the Tye it was two miles to the drive entrance and another mile uphill through parkland. Mistletoe hung in bunches on some of the old trees. Mr Goody, the butler, lived in the first lodge. Rumour had it that he placed all his mistress's bets for her at the races, but Mother tried not to gossip about it in front of us. We might be contaminated; but we knew she was quite well informed by her friend, Miss Wicks, Mrs Calverley's lady's maid, a friendly, regal figure in sable furs. We thought her very grand.

On arrival at the grounds Mother disappeared to help in the tea tent, run by the Women's Institute. Ruth and I were given trays of fresh buttonholes, hung on ribbons round our necks, and sent off to sell the buttonholes at sixpence each. We were meant to be appealing, dressed alike in our white cotton frocks and caps with pink ribbons. The buttonholes were soon all sold and we were free to roam the grounds and have rides on the swings or on the Shetland ponies, or to act as ball-boy for the tennis matches. We were on beautifully manicured lawns, so there was nothing so damaging or vulgar as roundabouts.

During the afternoon a brass band played rousing military marches on the lawn. I still find it difficult to resist falling into step when I hear such a band; I should have been the first to join an army recruiting procession if it had been led by a brass band. One of the joys of visiting the seaside was listening to the band.

Once Lord Baden-Powell visited the fête and spoke from the conductor's platform. Father had his straggly band of Matching

Down Hall, Matching, in the grounds of which the village fetes were held.

Boy Scouts on parade. They were a motley troop of fewer than a dozen whom Father attempted to drill, take camping, and train to be useful. He fought a losing battle with Mrs Calverley, who encouraged the Scouts and spoilt them, insisting on sending her luggage car to transport them wherever they went. He thought they should be brought up to be tough and to walk everywhere, carrying their packs on their backs. Mrs Calverley's kindness did not fit in with his idea of military discipline, nor a quasi-religious conviction that hardship improved the soul.

At eleven I became a Girl Guide, plump waist squeezed into a tight leather belt and a large, floppy hat stretched on my head. We were an odd tribe, wrestling with knots for which we found no use, making beds for housewifery badges, and galloping through country dances to a temperamental gramophone. Our aristocratic landlord's two elder daughters, Gladys and Phyllis, fresh from finishing school, ran the company. Regular meetings were handicapped by their gay social life, but they perservered with not very promising material. We thought them lovely to look at—one very fair, and one very dark. Moreover, the eldest gave us lifts in her car, a Renault at that.

We had spasmodic urges to try to win badges; usually we were

52

too disorganised to try. I was told to keep a nature diary and submit it for a Nature badge. Some months later I duly gave in my diary; it was quite unacceptable.

I was in the throes of discovering Matthew Arnold at school, and on some pages I was completely carried away, quoting chunks of *The Scholar Gipsy* or *Thyrsis*, revelling in the description of flowers, regardless of whether I had seen them or not. It was no way to approach a scientific study. The adjudicators were put completely off their stroke, and sent it back in despair with the suggestion that I should try for the Literature badge. I was much too discouraged and embarrassed to do so at once. However, I eventually handed in a pedestrian poem on some Greek classicial theme which I had written as a homework task for school. My teacher thought it was reasonably good.

Once more the adjudicators were nonplussed. The poem was handed back to me by my puzzled Captain with the comment that it was not good enough. I was sorry to let her down so badly; I never tried again.

August saw our Captain and Lieutenant installed at Kilmory Castle with a grouse-shooting party. A picture postcard arrived post-haste asking me to "take" the next meeting; they had forgotten to cancel it. It was a shambles, in spite of my loud voice; I was too short to be seen properly. However, the situation was saved by the gramophone played fortissimo; it kept us all lumping around in our country dances until we collapsed in perspiring exhaustion. I had done my good deed for the day.

We even went to camp. It poured with rain as we arrived, and I was promptly put on fatigue to carry pails of drinking water across a sodden field. The others huddled in tents, fortunately already erected as it was a permanent camp site at Thorpe-le-

Girl Guides ready to parade to Matching Church.

Soken. By now our beautiful fair-headed Lieutenant had made a socially-desirable marriage, and we had a new Guider from among her friends. She was tall and willowy, red-haired, with a slight stutter and a total inability to sing in tune. When we sat round the camp fire at night singing our hearty tunes and gesticulating wildly, she sat cross-legged beside us, droning monotonously to her feet. Camping must have been a drear business to her. All but one of us enjoyed it in spite of the weather; the exception was a shy village girl who had never been further than the next village and was completely overcome by homesickness. The only way to stem her tears was to return her to mother.

We once went as far as the Earl of Cadogan's seat at Bury St Edmunds for a rally at which we waited all day in the sun for the pleasure of walking past and saluting the Chief Guider, Princess Mary. We hardly saw her, but came home full of admiration for her pink-and-white English-rose complexion. Someone must have confided these details to us. The long coach ride to Bury and back was our greatest pleasure.

Very occasionally we took part in a church parade. It was more of a punishment than a privilege to carry the flag at the head of a dozen guides of all shapes and sizes. The weight of the pole and the awkward angle at which it was thought necessary to hold it with the right arm were killing.

After hay-making a village sports day attracted everyone in Matching. It was held in the meadow by the wood. Father with his parade ground voice organised the races. He scorned a megaphone.

The total lack of precision and urgency among the competitors bothered him. Everyone was so happy-go-lucky and casual that he was liable to become irritable by the end of the events. We learned to keep out of his way. However, he was able to relax while the youths climbed the greasy pole, and he only came into his own again to urge on the tug-of-war. We all liked to see someone drenched with water, so everyone gathered to watch the strong men push wheelbarrows carrying a mate, preferably a girl, who held a pole at arm's length in front of her ready to tilt a bucket of water suspended overhead. The pushers dived frantically forward to get clear, but they seldom avoided a soaking.

It was for the Coronation of King George VI that I remember Father organising his last sports event, this time a much more ambitious affair held on Matching Green. Times were changing. He shouted an order to a village lad to remove an obstruction. The lad stayed where he was, and flung back "We're not in the army now, you know."

A new generation had grown up. Father was out of his depth, and I pretended not to hear.

CHAPTER ELEVEN

Village Church

TO MY complete surprise, when we reached Churchgate School in Harlow Ruth and I were told we were "Devil Dodgers". This was because I had announced that we went to church *and* chapel; church in the morning with Father, and chapel in the evening with Mother. I omitted to say that Sunday school was sandwiched in between, in the afternoons. I was not aware that this would be considered an insurance policy against Hell; we simply enjoyed the variety.

Matching church was nearly two miles away from the Tye, standing on raised ground, surrounded by grassland, and reached by a private, unmade road along which we often had to pick our way carefully through the mud. The fifteenth-century vicarage and Matching Hall shared the same green, and in front of the church was a white plastered cottage, with the Marriage Feast Room above. This is a gem, also dating back to the fifteenth century, and one of only two such places in the country. It overhangs the cottage and is reached by a steep wooden staircase behind a duplicate front door. All parish meetings were held in this scrubbed wooden room, with its low ceiling, small-paned windows and bleached beams.

It must have been in use for five hundred years. Records show that it was once the village school room. Now the scouts trampled over it, the parochial church council argued there, and any willing volunteers practised there before setting off carol-singing, swinging lanterns and smelly bicycle lamps. The smell of these carbide lamps will always remain with me; we used them throughout our childhood, when bicycles were our only form of transport. It took some courage to tackle those lamps and cycle off to a meeting on dark, wet, winter evenings.

Every Sunday morning Father came downstairs immaculately dressed, usually in a navy-blue pin-striped suit and a red bow tie. He was ready to set off to church at 10.30 am. In the early years, on his return from the war, his military moustache was tightly waxed at the tips, but it gradually assumed softer proportions until no wax was used, and he adopted a characteristic smoothing motion with the knuckle of his forefinger so that it had merely a faint curve to each side. Ruth and I were looked over to make sure we had no holes in our socks, and if it was dry enough we set off across the fields to church.

This meant following a well-worn footpath which skirted a ditch, full of primroses in the spring, with clumps of peggles on the banks. Peggles was the Essex name for cowslips. The footpath changed sides for no apparent reason as we went along the edge of four fields, past ripening corn, or pink clover, and picked our way beside straight rows of swedes or mangold-wurzels. People still living then remembered the same footpath being used by bearers carrying coffins to funerals.

I loved the church bells urging us on. The bellringers were enterprising enough to ring the changes; the clear tone carried to all the surrounding hamlets, but the timing was unpredictable. Notes tumbled down on top of each other, followed by a breathless pause before the final cadence. We knew that one ringer among the group under the belfry at the back of the church always called the numbers evenly, because we listened to him if we were early in our pew; it was fascinating to guess who was responding slowly with his dancing bell-rope, and who was anticipating his call.

Church was quite a fashion parade. By tradition and tacit understanding the classes sat in carefully-defined pews— although none was actually labelled. Richer families were housed in the front pews in the nave; labourers kept discreetly to the back and side aisles. We sat in the middle of the church.

Father occasionally read the lesson, not really by choice. The vicar, Mr Brinkworth, was quietly spoken, and as he grew older and a sick man he found it a struggle to project his voice. It was so painful to listen to him that Father felt jolted, now and again, to relieve him.

He often dozed through the sermon, only to wake up and rub his hands noisily together as the last hymn was announced. We nudged him to try to forestall this embarrassing performance.

If we walked home by the road Mr Jones, our landlord, often offered us a lift in his open tourer car. Father always gaily refused with a wave of his hand. We thought his independence excessive; we would have welcomed the ride.

A group of four special pews behind the choir stalls and at right angles to the nave belonged to the folk from Down Hall. They were most conveniently placed for us all to marvel at the daring clothes and outrageous hats worn by the ladies. Mrs Calverley's escorts and house guests were colourful and exciting. Her voice and laugh were loud and mannish, and the village prattled about her doings. She created quite a stir by being the first person in the village to have a permanent wave. Lesser folk had water waves.

Since mother was friendly with her personal maid, Miss Wicks, Ruth and I were occasionally taken to tea at Down Hall; in the housekeeper's room, of course, presided over by Mrs Harper, the housekeeper. I was first introduced to a lavatory with a chain

St Mary's Church, Matching, where Mother and Father have lain for the last thirty years.

there, and was amazed at the rushing noises when I first pulled that chain. It was so frightening that no sense of decency could persuade me to close the door; I had to be able to bolt out the moment I had tugged it.

Several years later the elegant Miss Wicks married the head gardener, Mr Crowe, a widower, and went to live with him in the charming sixteenth-century dower house, along with his daughter, his blind mother, and a dwarf-like old man, an under-gardener, who flitted in and out and was known as Birdie.

The Howards from Matching Hall sat in the pew in front of us; this usually meant just Mrs Howard, as her husband was more at home riding his horse around the farm. He was a large red-faced man with an uncertain temper and a hook for a hand. This made him a slightly sinister figure to children; if he had a worn a patch over one eye we should have had no doubt that he was a pirate. He generally rode a beautiful Arab horse, slipping the reins through the hook.

His wife, a local JP, was short, plump and grey-haired, and loved by everyone. She sat in church with an ostrich feather lying on the brim of her hat, holding a lorgnette well away from her, poised over her prayer book. She drove a small governess cart and kept Shetland ponies for her grandchildren to ride. When they came to stay, Ruth and I were invited to join in treasure hunts, clock golf or croquet on the lawn.

I found Matins satisfying because it was set. I soon learned it all off by heart, and thought very little about what I was saying; I could speak the words and let my mind wander happily. I joined in the singing with gusto, but as I grew older I found myself stopped in my tracks when I suddenly realised that I was saying extraordinary words. I was not really attracted to Heaven if it was going to be all haloes, flowing with milk and honey, and if I had to play a harp; all that peace, too, and nothing to do. I had not come across metaphors then; but I still dislike that kind of hymn.

However, the organ had great appeal. Dora Brinkworth, an ARCO, who became my music teacher for many years, was the organist. At first the organ was pumped by hand by one of the

Dora Brinkworth, my music teacher for many years.

heftier choirboys, who pressed a wooden shaft up and down on the side of the organ in full view of the congregation, but later an electric pump was installed. There was a full choir of surpliced boys and men on both sides of the chancel; this would have been surprising if it were not generally agreed that some pressure was exerted on boys in "church" schools to turn up regularly for choir practice and Sunday services. No girls or women were ever invited.

The war memorial erected after the 1914–18 war was placed inside the main gate into the churchyard, with a sad list of well-known local names on it and a ring of rose bushes round the base. It was kept scrubbed and the roses were kept pruned by a rota of men in the village. More names from the same families were added in 1946. On the other side of the path is a large tomb to Dorothy Howard, the Howards' nurse daughter, who also died in the first World War.

Mother and Father have lain for the last thirty years by the fence at the far end of the churchyard, near groups of watching trees, overlooking undulating meadows and the lily pond in the hollow.

CHAPTER TWELVE

Chapel Affairs

CHAPEL services on Sunday evenings were much more
exciting than Matins at church. They were so unpredictable.
The minister for most of my childhood was Mr Walls, a jovial
retired city businessman, with a white Edward VII beard, a black
frock coat and false teeth which broke loose when he was excited.
We held our breath while he chased them round his mouth with
his tongue, and sighed with relief as he joggled them back into
position. He was a dramatic preacher given to loud crescendos,
wide-flung arms and thumps on his Bible. His prophecies were
alarming and I was never sure which dispensation we were living
in, even when he produced a lurid chart to illustrate the
successive dispensations and displayed it in front of the pulpit; but
I was quite sure I had to be saved to escape eternal damnation.

The hymns were Sankey and Moody—swinging emotional
tunes which we sang with enthusiasm. The minister was often so
carried away that before the last note had died away, he would
wave his hand with "Chorus again, friends!"—and we were off
once more with "Crown Hi-i-i-im, crown Hi-i-i-im!", ending in
great style with a magnificent rallentando. By the time I was
twelve I was often playing the American organ for the evening
service. This kind of service was most exciting; all stops out, feet
pumping the bellows, and myself singing above it all.

When Mrs Fenton, a farmer's wife, was playing the organ I
sometimes sang a solo. This was not because I had a beautiful
voice but because the aim was variety. Once Mr Smith of the
village shop, still sucking his teeth, gave out the notices
immediately after I had performed, and finished with the remark,
"She'll make a good 'socialist' when she grows up." Farmers in the
congregation, staunch Conservatives to a man, found this an
hilarious slip of the tongue; it was truer than they guessed.

Sometimes Dorothy Parish, a lonely girl who lived alone with
her old father, sang duets with me; but this was not a success. We
never rehearsed; each felt she knew the correct pace. I stuck
loudly and solidly to the tune, while she pitched her very sweet
voice slightly sharp. The congregation winced, and my mother
was once known to put her hands over her ears. The minister's
wife remonstrated with her afterwards, but she was unrepentant;
and we were finally discouraged.

By the time I was sixteen I had given up singing solos, too, because Mrs Fenton had such odd ideas of suitable hymns. We reached the limit when she chose for me "Where is my wandering boy tonight?" I firmly refused.

In order to visit his scattered flock Mr Walls invested in a second-hand tricycle, a heavy model, difficult to start; but after a few energetic turns on the pedals he was soon careering gaily along the road, back straight, pale grey Homburg firmly on his head. He could even take one hand off and wave to us. We followed him with fascinated admiration, hoping he would offer us a lift. He did. We stood on the back rail in turn, gripping his shoulders, and off he went on a slightly less certain course.

In the end he let us ride it. This was a complete fiasco. After a few turns of the pedals, every effort took us straight to the ditch. We refused to give in; but each time the left-hand verge proved a fatal attraction. Mother tried. She was equally unsuccessful, and equally frustrated.

Father thought this a ridiculous exhibition. He explained patiently to us that we must not try to balance as on a bicycle; just sit comfortably on the saddle and go straight ahead. We suggested that he should show us. He tackled it with confidence—and also ended up in the ditch on the left. Apparently the ability to ride a bicycle was a supreme handicap. The minister was cock-a-hoop, and rode swiftly round the Tye just to show us. We almost willed him to fall off, but obviously the Lord was on his side.

His wife was short and gentle, and very frail. She wore greys and mauves, ropes of beads and velvet toques decorated with flat pansies, and she carried chain handbags. Mr Walls always referred to her as "Mother". She was boss. She sat with Mother in

Left: Mr Walls, centre, on one of the many chapel outings.

Opposite page: Another chapel event, with Mrs Walls, centre, Mr Walls standing on the left of the back row, and Mother sitting in the front row, third from right.

the back pew in chapel, and if her husband's sermons went on too long, out came her handkerchief, which she draped over the back of the pew in front of her. He quickly took the hint and rounded off his tirade.

Festivals in chapel were cosy affairs. At harvest time Ruth and I were sent into the lanes to find berries and leaves for decoration. Commons and Wantz Lanes were lined with tall hedges full of a variety of different shrubs and trees; a sure sign of their early origins. We picked at random. In spite of their villainous thorns, we cut sprays of scarlet hips and clusters of dark-red haws with our penknives. It was enchanting to find a spindleberry bush; they were rare, and we hardly dared to pick them, but we stopped to wonder at the delicate branches of dangling pink spindle-berries, some already splitting to reveal their curious orange fruit inside, their grey-green pointed leaves dropping fast.

We always came back laden with long strands of bryony, covered with balls of fluffy seeds. Mother called it Travellers' Joy, but we called it Old Man's Beard. We twined it round the metal bars which crossed horizontally under the pitched roof of the chapel. From these rods hung paraffin lamps on chains, dangling above the centre aisle of coconut matting.

When I was very young a tortoise stove halfway down one wall was the only heating, but later several upright cylinder-shaped Valor Perfection paraffin stoves stood precariously down the centre aisle.

Normally the chapel was an ugly building of one large room, with pulpit and organ on a dais and a small vestry behind. Now it was transformed. Benches at ascending levels in front of the

pulpit were covered with a sheet and a profusion of vegetables and fruit piled on them. In the centre was a specially baked loaf in the shape of a sheaf of corn, the work of Mr Scott of Potter Street, and clustered round it were apples, potatoes, carrots, pumpkins, marrows, swedes, Michaelmas daises, dahlias and asters; two sheaves of corn stood like sentinels on either side. Above them, pinned to the centre of the velvet cover of the reading desk, was a large bunch of black grapes, and on each side bowls of late roses.

The centrepiece of grapes was a gesture of courtesy to the chairman of the harvest festival service, Mr Balfour from Moor Hall, who always sent them. He was invited to take the chair not because of his strong religious fervour but because he was benevolently inclined and invited the Sunday school to hold their annual treat in his grounds. The service was a grand affair; Mr Walls had the happy knack of persuading influential local people to participate. Doubtless he had an eye on the substantial increase in the collection; but he could justify anything if it furthered the Lord's work.

It was a warm occasion. We were intoxicated by the heady smell of ripe fruit and nearly suffocated by the stale smell of bodies. All the Sunday school children attended, hoping to receive a book prize for good attendance during the year. These were distributed during the service; innocuous romantic tales with a religious bias, published by Nelson, but none of them classics. However, they were eagerly competed for because they were something to read, and our homes had a dearth of children's books.

Next day came anticlimax; we had to tear down the decorations, burn the curling leaves and distribute or sell off the produce.

Easter weekend was another eagerly anticipated festival at chapel, chiefly for its social attractions rather than its religious implications. Mother always made herself, Ruth, and me new clothes for the Good Friday tea in the Women's Institute Hall next door to the chapel. Farmers from some miles around were regular members of the congregation, and their wives presided at the end of each long trestle table or coped with the urns of tea. The tables were laden with home-made cakes and scones—splits as the Cornish people called them; and several of the local farmers were Cornish in origin. Essex was good farming land and at the beginning of the century attracted many families from the less productive West Country.

Local celebrities were invited to address the afternoon meeting, and since this was in lighter vein it was considered suitable to invite a woman; so much the better if she had a double-barrelled name. She could be relied on to be amusing, gently stimulating, and to put a note in the collection. The chapel was crowded; we liked our dose of glamour. For Good Friday was quite as gay as

Easter Sunday. Calvary was certainly mentioned and the message of the Cross expounded, but the true implications of the event were lost on us. The spirit was of resurrection; death was hurriedly dismissed. We knew what it was like to live in the dark of winter; Easter brought new hope, and we were ready to welcome it as soon as possible. For months now our parents had been preoccupied with paraffin lamps to be filled and trimmed each morning, with emptying grates of ash, continually collecting and sawing up wood, and stumbling into dark tunnels along cheerless unlit roads at night. The days had closed in quickly and we had lived with lamplight and candlelight too long. We couldn't wait till Easter day.

Christmas was more of a family affair. It would have smacked of Popish tricks to have enacted a Nativity play in church or chapel. No parallels were drawn between the birth of a baby two thousands years ago and a present birth. Yet country people would have understood. Birth was often lonely in poor, even sordid, surroundings. Some babies were illegitimate, too; but it was all too dangerous to dwell on. So we grew up with our tidy pigeon-holed Bible stories, sentimentally viewed from a safe distance.

Christmas became identified with its gay trappings. It was a time for carol-singing and a party in the Institute Hall with a Christmas tree, and an orange to take home. We sat in a circle and played "Spinning the Trencher" and "Winking"; we danced the Veleta, the Polka and Sir Roger de Coverley; and we acted charades and sometimes were entertained by a conjurer. At home we pinned notes on our bedroom door so that Father Christmas would know where we were sleeping. We were not convinced of his arrival down a chimney, but we played the game so as not to disillusion our parents, who went to elaborate lengths to perpetuate the myth.

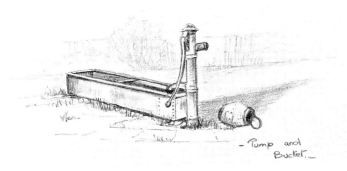

— Pump and
Bucket —

63

Presentation to Mrs Salmon.
By the Matching Nursing Association
on 14. October 1925
In recognition of valuable services
rendered as Honorary Secretary for
eight years — And the warmest thanks
accorded her by the following suscribers :—

M^{rs}. P. Silcock. Mrs Frank. H. Jones. M^{r} & Mrs Billings & family.
M^{rs} & Mrs Stephens. Mrs John Howard. (Pres:) Mrs J. Seymour.
Mrs Scanttebury. Miss Nicholls. Mrs Garrard.
Mrs J. F. Saville. Miss Churchman. Mrs F. Baker.
Mrs Curry. Mrs Tom Howard. M^{rs}. C. Robertson.
Mrs Taylor. Mrs Griffin. M^{rs}. A. Dellar.
M^{rs}. W. Peacock. Mrs Rule. M^{rs}. A. Judd.
Mrs Sanford. Mrs King. M^{rs}. J. Footitt.
M^{rs} & Mr Hawkins. Miss. L. Simmonds. Mrs Rowland.
Mrs Davies. Miss Hazelwood. Mrs Porter.
M^{rs}. John Smith. M^{rs}. T. Billings. Mrs Jackson.
a friend. M^{rs}. W. Smith. Mrs G. Rixon.
M^{rs}. J. Ellis. Mrs Hammond. Mrs Crabbe.
M^{rs}. A. Butcher. M^{rs}. Mison. M. Tye.

CHAPTER THIRTEEN

Doctors and the District Nurse

THE MANSE beside the chapel was on the fringe of the Tye, on the road to Matching Green, a much larger collection of houses about two miles away.

There was only one house along the road, almost midway between the two villages. Everyone knew it. There it was on a sharp corner, one storey high, octagonal in shape, but known as the Round House—and it smelt. If the wind was blowing your way, an unmistakable sour smell met you yards away. It permeated the clothes of the family of children who lived there; among them, Lily, quiet and gentle, the eldest; Reggie, silent and clumsy; and Wilfred, red-haired, round-faced and grinning. No-one wanted to sit next to them at Sunday school for fear of fleas; they had those little red spots round the back of their necks.

Many people tried to help them to keep warm with parcels of cast-off clothing, but the parents were hopelessly inadequate at managing and nothing seemed to make much difference to the children's appearance for very long. The mother was like an apathetic version of Milly Molly Mandy's mother; tall, with a bun on top of her head and an apron tied tightly round her middle. The father was an inarticulate farm labourer working for Mr Howard at Matching Hall.

All the children smiled shyly and said little. They did not join the other village boys in their usual escapades, nor had they the initiative to get into trouble. It seemed an affectionate family, not even resenting its poverty, just defeated by conditions beyond its control.

Social services as we know them now were non-existent. The family was caught in the trap, with father walking to work and working too hard physically to have the extra energy needed to cultivate a good garden of vegetables and unable to buy enough protein to feed a growing family. Old men tell me now that as children they had to catch sparrows at weekends so that their mothers could make a meat pie. I think most of them kept a few chickens scratching in the yard and fed them on scraps, eating them on special occasions.

A certificate presented to Mother by the
Matching Nursing Association.

The meeting places for most of the men in the evenings were the village pubs; not smart carpeted places as we know them now, serving good food and catering for the mobile middle class, but dull bare rooms with sawdusted floors, smelling of smoke and stale beer. There were two on the Tye: the *Hare and Hounds* and the *Fox*. Both are still there, completely transformed and welcoming an affluent new public.

Father would not have gone inside them then, and Mother thoroughly disapproved of such dens of iniquity. They catered entirely for labourers, gipsies, a few women regarded as somewhat dissolute, and packs of thirsty London cyclists pedalling through the countryside at weekends. The *Fox* was separated from Woodville by only a meadow, so we were aware of its noisier evenings.

This was the favourite haunt of an old woman who worked seasonally on the land and was known to everyone as Aunt Tilly. She lived in a tumbledown black-boarded cottage at the end of a muddy overgrown lane. It was squalid, and for all her good humour she was squalid too. Everyone knew she behaved scandalously, but no-one attempted to interfere.

She arrived at every rummage sale with several inconspicuous empty bags, and they were filled at lightning speed before the sale had really begun. The organisers never ceased to be amazed at the rate she went round all the stalls, deftly taking anything which might be useful or which she might be able to sell; but they did nothing. She was an institution.

In the evenings and at weekends she would be at the *Fox*, bundled up in her dirty clothes, but in the warm, leading a sing-song which grew more off-key as the evening wore on. At the height of the entertainment the noise reached us. Mother tossed her head in disapproval.

Tilly did not always reach home at night. It was a long way, the road was dark and her gait was uncertain. It was easier to lie by the roadside till morning.

I once made a fool of myself at the *Hare and Hounds*. I was an inquisitive child and sometimes Mother dodged answering my questions; once in a mischievous mood she let me call at the public house specifically to ask the plump daughter of the house if the small boy running around, evidently illegitimate, was hers. She was deeply suspicious.

"Does he belong to you?" I asked. "Who's his Daddy?"

"Who sent you?"

"Mummy! She wouldn't tell me, so she told me to ask you."

"You clear orf!"

Mother let us down badly another time. Ruth and I dearly wanted a brother and persistently demanded one. Mother sent us to the family doctor to ask about it. Two brothers, Doctors Newcomb and Tom Day, both bachelors, lived in Harlow in a large Georgian house on Mulberry Green. Newcomb looked rather like a conventional civil servant and practised chiefly in Harlow; Tom, our doctor, was a delightful eccentric. He was a familiar figure in the village, sailing through in the back of an open tourer, driven by a chauffeur in a peaked cap, navy-blue livery and gaiters. He wore a deer-stalker hat on his tightly curled hair and a weighty tweed coat with a layered cape, exactly like Sherlock Holmes.

Ruth and I must have been ten and eight then, for we rode to Harlow on our bicycles, waited in the surgery for about an hour and then were ushered into the consulting room. I came straight to the point; and he laughed at us. He thought it was a huge joke, but we failed to see it. He must have sensed our dismay at last, because he promised to do his best and we hurried home full of hope. Nothing came of it.

We had no surgery in the village, and it was too far to go into Harlow for most visits, so all the village rejoiced in home visits from the doctor, a situation which lasted until I was grown up. Dr Tom hated the strong scent of flowers. One day he came into the dining room, where Mother had put a bowl of Madonna lilies. Without a word he swept out and settled himself in another room. Another time he picked the bowl of flowers up and stood it outside the front door.

When the Days retired a new young doctor came, with a completely different style. The whole village warmed to Norman Booth. He was skilled and conscientious, full of laughter and sympathy, wearing himself out to make life better for his poorer patients. He still had to visit our homes, and to many he brought not only medical but practical help. He lent a gramophone to one family, and brought a radio to cheer a sick young woman in the council houses who was depressed; and many others had cause to be grateful for his kindness. I was working at Chingford before I was married and came to visit my parents most weekends. Neither they nor I had a car. He insisted that I called at his home in Harlow on my way out, and as soon as surgery was over he would drive me to Matching. When my father died, Mother was bothered because she was crippled with arthritis and unable to get to the shops to buy black for the funeral. He put his arms round her shoulders and said, "Don't bother! Just go out as if you're going for a walk with him."

Our nearest hospital was Rye Street, Bishop's Stortford, little bigger than the usual cottage hospital, but everyday medical help came from the district nurse. She was a familiar sight, turning up on her bicycle for any emergency. The nurses were all friendly with Mother because she was a useful on-the-spot ally; she had no nursing qualifications but lots of common sense, and could be relied on to be unflappable in emergencies and to render simple first aid. She was for ever visiting someone on the Tye to apply a bandage or give advice on spots or croup. She adored "her" babies at the Infant Welfare Clinic, held in the Institute Hall once a month, a local amenity she ran for nearly thirty years.

I suspect she welcomed the district nurses at home because they gossiped to her. In our presence they often dropped their voices to a confiding whisper and nodded knowingly to each other. It was only years afterwards that I discovered what Nurse had meant by her horrific remark, "She says she's going to use a darning needle this time!"—a remark which brought forth a shocked reply from Mother, "What a stupid girl!"

Ruth and I kept our ears open and collected details of operations and snippets of information about a feeble-minded girl who lived with an old man, and comments on the squalor of some cottages. None of them remained in our minds for more than a few days; our own pursuits were much more interesting.

District nurses came and went: one was locally born, fat and homely, with a warm Essex accent; one was Welsh and married a village lad ten years her junior. We loved Nurse Harsley best. She was young and slim, with red-gold hair, and looked very pretty as she pedalled smartly by on her bicycle, navy-blue silk veil flying out behind her. She wore stiff white collars and cuffs and had the characteristic gesture of shooting her hands forward to make them comfortable before she drank a cup of tea. Ruth and I adored her as a figure of romance, and there was always a bigger congregation at the chapel on the evening when she was singing a solo.

Tongues wagged about her affairs, for every eligible male was pleased to be seen with her. When one of two brothers, bachelor farmers, committed suicide we understood that it was for love of her and jealousy of his brother's success in wooing. Strangely enough, she never married the remaining brother; she was young and he was already middle-aged. Who could blame her for flirting outrageously in a village lacking in many social amenities? Later, after she had moved to another district, she married a widower; a retired headmaster. We thought this very dull and unenterprising of her, and switched our adoration to worthier idols.

CHAPTER FOURTEEN

Village Blacksmith and Local Farms

THE TYE was the centre of our world. Matching Green was really much more important and much bigger, with many cottages spread round the perimeter of two large greens, bisected by several roads. There were not only cottages, but a sprinkling of substantial houses owned by families of some social standing, who supported a flourishing cricket team which maintained a well-kept cricket table and pavilion on the centre of the green and which attracted a faithful following from miles around. There was a large pond, too, with a colony of toads, particularly during the mating season.

We were even more attracted to the shop of the only local craftsman, Mr Saville, the blacksmith, whose smithy stood right on the far corner of the Green on the road to Hatfield Heath. Ruth and I would stand peering in at the door of his dark and cluttered forge, feeling the heat of his blazing fire and watching his sure, swift movements as he hammered and shaped the horseshoes, holding them in rough tongs in the flame if he needed them soft and malleable, or dipping them in cold water to harden them. We were a little nervous, but filled with admiration for the fearless way he rebuked a shy, bucking horse and, with his back to its flank, picked up its foot and rested it on his leather apron while he measured the hot shoe on its hoof. We were never quite sure that this operation, which produced a smell of scorched horn and a sizzling noise, was painless for the horse, and we were horrified to see the smart way he sliced off pieces of horn with a sharp knife to get a perfect fit before he nailed the shoe on with long handmade nails.

His only son, Horace, worked with him and took over the business when his father died. Horace was a shy and diffident young man with a ready smile and a nervous, high-pitched voice. As he spoke he patted a curl in place on his forehead; everyone mimicked him. He had learned his craft well, but the business gradually declined as farm horses gave way to tractors, and has now disappeared. Horace lived to be a lonely old man in a derelict cottage slowly disintegrating round him. The thatch was battered, weeds and shrubs choked the paths and the cottage had no services; but he must have felt the need to go on creating. Cement was cheap, so for many years he filled the front garden with larger-than-life concrete figures of well-known people. It was even rumoured that he made his own false teeth in cement. For years he stood at the gate of his cottage pointing out his statues of Sir Anthony Eden, the Duke of Edinburgh, the Queen Mother and Cliff Michelmore, among others. He had a pencil and pad in his hand and drew lightning sketches for visitors who drew up in their cars to stare. He signed them with a flourish—an artist manqué.

Another skilled craftsman was Mr Scott, the baker from Potter Street, near Harlow. A fat, red-faced, jolly man with a cap on the side of his head, he came round in his van to the villages once a week. He walked smartly down the garden path, whistling and leaning sideways to balance an immense basket full of fresh-smelling crusty loaves and rolls which he carried on his crooked arm. Strangely enough, we found that he too filled his garden with models; but his interests were landscapes with windmills and houses, all meticulously executed. His garden was a landmark on the main road through from Harlow to Epping. Evidently his modelmaking brought no lasting satisfaction, for years ago we learned that he had committed suicide.

The men ploughing in the fields were skilled, too. In all weathers they trudged behind teams of horses with sacks over their shoulders, guiding the plough along straight furrows; lines of young crops in the spring bore witness to their keen eye. They cared for their horses, polishing their brasses and plaiting their manes and tails with coloured braids, happy to compete in ploughing matches in the neighbourhood in their spare time.

Few farms need their skills now, and a strange loneliness has overtaken farm workers. Tractors and increasingly sophisticated farm machinery have not only altered their status but decreased their numbers to such an extent that where we used to see a bunch of men hoeing in a field, then shouldering their tools and walking home together, we now find one lonely man on a machine with nobody to communicate with, no-one even in sight; and often he will continue working with floodlights far into the night. It is a cause for concern to some farmers.

In the Twenties the life of the village was of necessity geared to the land and the seasons. When potato-picking began, the village school regularly closed for a holiday. The women, old and young, went into the fields and spent all day at their backbreaking job, up and down the rows, keeping together for company and taking their babies in ramshackle prams on to the fields with them. School children helped their mothers to fill their pails, keep an eye on the babies and add a little to their meagre earnings.

Pea-picking was a rather more colourful time because it heralded the arrival of the gipsies. Horse-drawn caravans, broken-down vans, clothes' lines of washing and an odd assort-

Edie and Evelyn Fenton outside Shetlocks Farm, Matching Tye.

ment of bent containers and cooking utensils littered the entrance
to the pea-fields, guarded by a lean mangy lurcher tied to a stake,
barking at everyone walking along the road. We were surprised to
see in most of the caravans gaily coloured china and bunches of
bright artificial flowers. The adults seemed roughly affectionate to
a number of dark-eyed grubby children, squabbling and tireless.
We found them a fascinating diversion, but were told that they
never went to school. The gipsies picked all day, visited our homes
selling home-made pegs in their spare time, and earned the
reputation of stealing the odd chicken. Because of this some
farmers refused to employ them.

Essex land is heavy and fertile, and the farmers became
increasingly affluent. Ruth and I visited all the farms in the area
and knew the families well. Almost opposite Woodville on the Tye
is Shetlocks Farm, where the Fentons lived with their six
children; all but one boy and a girl, Frank and Evelyn, seemed
grown-up to us. Every afternoon we took a big jug to the back door
to be filled with milk for tuppence. There were no rules and
regulations about conditions in cowsheds and Tuberculin Tested
herds: we had the milk warm and frothy straight from the cow.

If the men had been shooting there might also be a rabbit for
sixpence.

Evelyn was a bosom friend, sharing our secrets, joining in all
our games and walking with us for miles across the fields and
along the lanes, always looking for new ways of making circular
tours round the villages. Frank cycled to Harlow College every
day, and it was not until we were in our teens that we got to know
him when we shared a tennis court in the field beside us. In

71

Harlow College, to
which Frank cycled
every day. Later Ruth
worked at the college
as an assistant
secretary.

practice, that meant that Frank and his elder brother Ted cut and
rolled it, while we made wobbly lines on ground made uneven by
moles persistently heaving up mounds. Hazards added to the fun;
but the multitude of gnats mourning over the ditch which
separated us from the wood was not so amusing.

Inside, Shetlocks was very like Woodville, except that they had
dogs curled up on a sagging settee and a strong smell of cigars.
Mother had weaned Father off cigarettes and tobacco on to Heath
and Heather's herb tobacco, so we were used to a pot-pourri-
scented smoke around the house. Not that Father really liked it;
but it was easier to give in to Mother's insistence that tobacco was
bad for him, and he still smoked a furtive cigarette with a wink at
us if Mother was busily engaged.

Across Matching Green, past Silcock's Post Office and General
Store, was a road through to The Roothings, now called The
Rodings. A five-barred gate and a long drive led to Stock Hall, a
moated sixteenth-century farmhouse, where Sam and Bessie
Stephens lived. They were an elderly Cornish couple, warm and
welcoming, and oddly matched in appearance. He was rough and
ready; she was smartly dressed and with a definite presence. They
had rich Cornish accents and a delightful misuse of pronouns. "Us
am coming," he would say, "if you'll just wait two-three minutes."

He rattled through the village in his old Ford tourer, hood up
but no sides, so open to all the draughts, driving dangerously fast
but with a warning clatter that could be heard at a considerable
distance. We often wondered if his sight was good enough; it was
long before the days of driving tests. Fortunately there was very
little traffic, only vulnerable cyclists.

His wife took us into her warm kitchen with tall dark settles against the walls and low-beamed ceiling. She plied us with delicious splits while we listened to her tales of life on their Cornish farm when she was young; her parents fed and housed large numbers of journeymen labourers during harvest time each year and the women of the house had their work cut out to cook enough food to satisfy their enormous appetites. It sounded like a continuous baking spree.

The Hawkins, relations of the Stephens and also Cornish, farmed Housham Hall on the Harlow side of the village. This is also a lovely old manor house, mentioned in Domesday Book as Oversham Manor. It became like a second home to Ruth and me. Mr Hawkins had been in business in London before he bought the farm and made a flourishing concern of it; but they were unpretentious, kind people, almost amazed to point out to me the old chest of drawers in the kitchen which had once been a valued piece of furniture in their bedroom. Now a uniformed maid kept her tablecloths and dusters in its drawers.

Housham Hall

In the pantry there were always splits, Cornish pasties and yellow saffron buns, and in the dairy huge pans of clotted cream and pats of butter.

They came to the village chapel on Sunday evenings, and I stood fascinated beside Mrs Hawkins as she harmonised the hymns in a strong contralto voice. Their daughter Hilda, ten years older than me, gave me piano lessons until she married. Bottom drawers were an essential part of a bride's equipment, and many were the times in the late Twenties that I would turn up for a game of tennis with her, only to find her determined to do the eight rows of crochet for a tablecloth border which she had set herself as a daily task, and I had to spend half an hour cheering her on before we could play.

When she married Edgar Tinney, one of the sons of John Tinney, of Thorley Hall, a well-known Essex farmer, she and her husband took over Housham Hall and the Hawkins retired to Harlow. The farm became a large business, embracing several other farms as it increased and affording work for many local farm labourers. Throughout the year they employed eight men on the home farm, never standing them off at slack times, and were very much respected for their excellent labour relations.

Both Edgar and his father-in-law owned little Morris two-seaters with a dicky; we loved to ride in them. However, I can remember when I was a little younger being delighted to ride with Mr Hawkins in his pony and trap to Bishop's Stortford along the old A11 from Harlow, on one of his trips to market on Thursday mornings. On the way we met a steamroller with a party of roadmenders, one of whom came forward to lead the pony past as he shied nervously on approaching the hissing engine.

Old Granary.
on staddles.

CHAPTER FIFTEEN

Country Walks and the Point-to-Point

WHEN we tired of the farms we turned again to the wood, so near and enticing. Mother would join us for an evening stroll after a hot summer day. The wood was regular in shape, with wide tracks meeting at crossroads in the middle. Father foraged there often, collecting the dry, fallen young trees and dragging them across the ditch into the chicken run, and then sawing them up to store in the wood shed between the privy and the wash-house.

A large bush of syringa leaned over the entrance to the main path through the wood. The scent was heavy on the air all summer. By autumn it was waning, and we were attracted to the hazel hedge beside it. No-one had hacked it down for years, and we picked the rough rounded leaves and stripped them to skeletons, our fingers just fitting the regular distances between the ribs. We filled our pockets with bunches of hazel nuts, now ripe in their jagged sheaths.

Some days we heard the huntsman's horn and knew that the Essex Hunt was following the scent of a fox through the wood. We hurried so as not to miss the chase. This was a favourite haunt of theirs, and we could see them easily along such straight wide tracks.

Once a fox dashed into our chicken run in desperation and, amid startled squawks, dived into the chicken house, which had once been a stable. It cowered in a corner among the hens nesting in the mangers; the hunt surrounded us, and Father latched the door. The huntsman dismounted and some minutes later presented Mother with a fox's brush, which decorated the kitchen for many years. We had only a passing qualm at the incident; chickens were precious and we had lost several to the fox. Within minutes the hunt had left us and moved to Man Wood, near Matching Green, on a fresh scent.

Before they were given a permanent site in Essex, and before the new council houses spread over more fields around the Tye, the hunt's point-to-point races were held at Matching, and the starting and finishing post were in Mr Fenton's meadow opposite Woodville. Ruth and I were determined not to miss a thing; it caused tremendous excitement for days. From the front bedroom windows we could see the marquees, the betting booths, the fences and entrances being erected. Farmers lent their waggons for grandstands. Most of the races were out of sight, across hedges, suitably trimmed and reinforced, and across the fields beyond; but we had no need to stir to savour the excitement and to watch the busy scene of horse-boxes arriving, horses being exercised, and hundreds of people from miles around flocking to the course to watch the fun. Matching was on the map.

Mrs Fenton put on her best cloche hat of parma violets with a little veil and a new frock and gloves; she was invited to a champagne lunch in one of the marquees. We chatted about such grandeur; but Mother disapproved. She stayed resolutely indoors while we did our best to see as much as possible.

Mr Walls, from the chapel, felt it his duty to evangelise; he braved the racegoers on the course with an open-air meeting, handing out suitable leaflets to remind them that they were on their way to Hell. How my grandmother would have approved! Ruth and I were embarrassed for him; we were fond of him and didn't like his earnestness being spurned.

Mother's chief annoyance was the number of folk who came up the garden path and asked to use our lavatory. It was all very well

Rule's Cottage · Housham

for the council house tenants to put up notices offering a "Wash and Brush-up, 2d.", but she had no desire to make money out of our privy, and certainly they were not coming indoors.

Tom Howard from Kingstons, son to Mr and Mrs Howard of Matching Hall, was well known for his performances at the point-to-point. He was accident prone, and it added to the local interest if he was thrown at a jump and broke his collar bone.

His wife, Hilda Howard, the life and soul of the village, ran local events with vigour and a noisy sense of humour. She was treasurer of the Women's Institute, and everybody's friend. She strode energetically about, cardigan resting on top of an ample protruding behind, wearing sensible stockings and shoes, constantly sticking hairpins back into her wayward bun of thick hair. She was one of the first people in the village to own a car—a grey Morris Cowley with a dicky. After having her windscreen broken, she dumbfounded the village by driving madly through at all of thirty miles an hour with a plank of wood in its place; we stepped smartly out of her way. She and Tom had no children, but many relations. She came from the well-known miller's family, the Edwards of Bishop's Stortford, and persuaded F. C. Edwards to sing at some of the village concerts. She went to great trouble to entertain her nieces and nephews when they came to visit her; Ruth and I were invited too, and particularly enjoyed her treasure hunts all over the garden and farm. The "Vale of Tears" stumped us, until we chanced on a lane where she had hung onions from the trees.

Ruth, Evelyn and I knew just where to look in the lanes and meadows at all seasons to find a particular flower or plant. We were not very knowledgeable on names, as we had no beautifully illustrated nature reference books then, only Arthur Mee's *Children's Encyclopedia*, and that meant searching through several volumes to compare drawings, but we could recognise all the common ones.

We found late summer and autumn the most rewarding seasons for wandering. Larks hung in the sky, pouring out their song; sometimes a flock of lapwings settled on the field with their plaintive "pee-wit" call, lifting restlessly into the air again as we approached. Sometimes we were lucky enough to see a magpie, or better still, two; we knew it was two for joy.

Along the verges and ditches we could smell the almond scent of meadowsweet, standing erect with its creamy, feathery flowers. We took home our offerings of hot bunches of yellow Tom Thumbs, cherry pie, white starry bachelor's buttons and purple climbing vetch. We couldn't resist picking the large white convolvulus bells tangled in the hedge, but they drooped to a wet grey rag before we reached home.

In the hedges, often uncut, we found the wayfaring trees, with their berries of black, red and green, pushing their tough stems forward between maple bushes aflame with scarlet and yellow leaves. The leaves were turning purple on the red stems of the dogwood.

Sometimes we made a collection of grasses. They abounded: soft, sand-coloured tops, green upright spikes like bellropes covered with seeds, thousands of slender stems with dark drooping heads, others stiff and erect with red feathery tops swaying gently—a reddish-brown haze when seen in the distance. We cropped their heads desultorily, plucking alternate seeds off to "He loves me, he don't . . ." or tucking the broken-off tops of thick-headed ones into the stem and, as we tossed them in the air, chanting

> "Grandmother, grandmother,
> Jump out of bed.
> Your house is on fire
> And your children all dead."

We were not aware of any macabre sentiments, just as we saw no sinister meaning in *Alice in Wonderland*.

We often ate berries; the fleshy skin of the hips, discarding the furry seeds inside; and all but the centre stone of the haws, which we called bread-and-cheese. Other berries were not for eating; all country children had heard dire warnings against touching the brilliant berries of the woody nightshade.

We stopped to talk to anyone working in the fields or pottering around a cottage garden, we inquiried after the sick, and we gratefully accepted some fruit or a cup of water. There were so many folk of the same name: Whitbreads, Byfords, Hockleys, Peacocks, Seymours—closely intermarried families. Father learned most of these relationships over the years, because he started and ran for many years a Men's Club in the Institute Hall. He took care of their savings each week; and when outings or Christmas came it was amazing how much they had saved in small sums.

The Club, which met on Monday evenings, provided darts, cards, snooker and billiards, organised matches and tournaments, and served refreshments. It was a meeting place other than a pub; no woman was allowed, even to help by washing up; the members were self-sufficient. Father cycled to Harlow every Monday afternoon to buy a large slab of fruit cake which he cut into equal slices with careful attention and mathematical precision, so that he was sure to make a profit on the sale to swell the funds. We watched the operation with fascinated concern.

CHAPTER SIXTEEN

London Grandparents

THE TALL HOUSE in Digby Road, East London, where my father's parents, Louisa and Henry Salmon, lived is a vague grey building to me, just like the others beside it, with no flowers, only evergreen shrubs in the front garden. Perhaps Ruth and I were taken on a visit only once or twice before the crash came; we were certainly very young.

The front door was under an arch at the side, and the drawing room was upstairs; it struck us as a very odd arrangement. The furniture was dark and grand, and the china precious. A heavy red curtain was looped back in the doorway. There were so many stairs; the kitchen was down in the basement, and the dining room on the ground floor.

Grandma Salmon was soft and plump, with slippery skirts, lace jabots and pretty white wavy hair. She always wore jewellery: gold brooches with Grandpa's miniature on the back, lockets on long gold chains opening to reveal oval photographs, dangling earrings and an intriguing button with lorgnette attached; as a special favour we were initiated into the art of pulling the chain out for use and letting it whirr back into a coil inside the button. I mimicked everyone for the family's entertainment; Grandma was my favourite subject.

Grandpa was white-haired and thin, a shadowy figure with his long face and drooping, sad moustache. I can remember him only in a black velvet jacket, occasionally sporting an embroidered blue-tasselled velvet smoking cap, which survived for years in my children's dressing-up box.

My father was the apple of their eye. They had planned that he should carry on their business, a livery tailor's. Grandpa started the firm in Huntingdon, where my father was born and attended the Old Grammar School. Oliver Cromwell had been a pupil at that school. I still have Father's terse school reports, beginning with "Could work harder" and going on to "Excellent" as he grew older. The only photograph we had of him among his school mates had his head carefully scratched out: everyone was wearing a mortarboard and he thought he looked ridiculous. He sometimes talked of his schooldays: teaching was very formal, with a High Master and Monitors; desks were tall and heavy, and the windows too high to see out of. This was the last half of the nineteenth

Grandma Salmon wearing a lace jabot held in place by a gold brooch. She always wore jewellery.

Grandpa Salmon wearing his black velvet jacket but not his blue-tasselled smoking cap.

century and grammar schools still concentrated on the Classics. When I was learning Latin more than fifty years later he could quote accurately pages of Virgil—an astonishing sidelight on someone we thought we knew as a quiet, unambitious army man.

Their business went well and they moved to London, Grandpa employing a staff of cutters and tailors. My father grew up to be a gay young man-about-town, acquiring a large repertoire of popular music hall songs. His cousin George, who accompanied him on his jaunts, was a mythical figure to us, since we heard of him only subsequently in Father's more expansive moods.

For many years Father, who rose early at Matching and usually sat on the back doorstep drinking tea and contemplating the wood, would burst into song, particularly as he began to strop his cut-throat razor on the leather strap behind the back door, assuring us that "It takes a man to sing in the morning, any silly fellow can sing at night." The tunes were always those from the music halls such as *The Man who Broke the Bank at Monte Carlo*, *Let's All Go Down the Strand* and, when he was feeling

Father's first school report, Huntingdon Grammar School, 1881.

sentimental, *In the Shade of the Old Apple Tree* or *You are my Honeysuckle, I am the Bee.*

The one song which, for some unknown reason, reduced him to tears of laughter when we sat on his knee in the evening and demanded a song was *Don't Have Any More, Mrs Moore!* We thought the humorous appeal was overrated, but we were delighted to see him mop his eyes helplessly and spurred him on to further extravagances until we too were rolling around with laughter. Perhaps Cousin George could have explained.

Apparently Grandpa cherished hopes that Father would add a new dimension to the retail side of the business, and apprenticed him to a well-known outfitters in Holborn. When it came to massaging tight kid gloves over the fingers of young ladies, Father revolted; it was no man's job. He lied about his age, joined the army and was sent to the Boer War. Grandpa bought him out.

Later, because he steadfastly refused to shop life and became rather ashamed of his gayer exploits with Cousin George, he was allowed to join the Royal Horse Artillery and was stationed on the North-West Frontier in India for about seven years.

When business was good Grandpa was expansive and acquired a carriage and pair, buying Grandma extravagant clothes and presents. He was improvident, too, so that when the days of liveries declined he had no savings; he finally went bankrupt and they came to live with us in Matching. This was after Father came home from the First World War, and when we were small children.

81

Grandpa was still resplendent in his velvet jacket, and Grandma ventured out on a fine day for a short walk through the village swathed in a fur coat and leaning on a silver-topped stick. Such luxuries were unheard of; Mother hinted indignantly that they even drank port in their room.

They brought only a few treasures with them; one or two inlaid boxes, several brass-cornered walnut box writing desks, half a dozen pale watercolours and two still-life oils by an uncle, a beautiful grandfather clock, an oval inlaid dining table, a large walnut tallboy and some precious china stored on a "what-not". It was little enough saved from their treasures, but the bedroom which we spared them at the back of the house was crowded.

The bentwood and cane rocking chair came too. Most of the day Grandma sat by the log fire in the dining room rocking gently, a fine Paisley shawl round her shoulders, her feet on a hassock. Her fingers were often white and numb and she sat rubbing them quietly. Beside her she had the large leather-bound family Bibles and photograph albums with heavy gilt locks. We never tired of looking at these albums and the pictures they contained of strange bewhiskered men, women with bustles and puffed-up hair, and stiffly posed family groups with pots on stands and looped curtains as a suitable background. We learned to know them all, though we never met any of them: Grandma's world was peopled with them, but they never came to visit her in the country.

Grandma Salmon with Mother, Father, Ruth and me outside Woodville.

Grandpa died first, and Grandma dressed in deepest black for the rest of her life; for the first few months black veiling trailed from her hat. She was the only person I can remember in widow's weeds.

In such an inconvenient house as Woodville the arrival of my grandparents must have added a great burden on my energetic little mother; she coped with all the extra work. They marvelled at her capable housekeeping, but were too old to help. Both died of heart attacks at the house. Doctors and hospitals were too far away to reach in time; my parents had no car and no telephone until we were grown up. The only village telephone was not even in a kiosk but inside the village shop, unusable at night.

Ruth and I shared a bedroom next to our grandparents, and when Mother called us one morning with the news that Grandma had died in the night, we said simply, "We know; we heard," and pulled the bedclothes over our ears.

Father had one sister, Alice, who lived at home. She came to live with us in the country too. She was tall and slim, with fair curly hair and good features. Father was fond of her; we thought her kind but aloof, and her face was often sad. She really had no great love for children, so we kept out of her way as much as possible. She was educated to be just an ornament; no one expected her to earn her own living, and she had no qualifications nor desire to do so. When the crash came, she was the biggest casualty. She had learned to play the piano and brought piles of music, mostly "Studies", with her. I still have some of them, but I don't remember her ever performing on our piano.

Her pet spaniel, Nigger, came too, and added to Mother's minor irritations. Alice and Mother merely tolerated each other. Mother resented her uselessness and pettish, pouting manner; Alice resented the fall in the family fortunes, and was jealous of her brother's wife. She was not likely to marry now, and when after her parents' death she made attempts to earn a living as housekeeper to another maiden lady in Grange Road, Bishop's Stortford, she was sadly inadequate.

Less than ten years later she died of cancer at our house, Mother nursing her devotedly; but only Father really loved her, and there was no opportunity for the rest of us to do so now.

Before Ruth and I left for school one morning we were taken into the bedroom to say "Goodbye" to her. Mother seemed to think this was a necessary ritual. She was pale and emaciated, and the air was drenched with eau-de-cologne; I still dislike the smell. We dutifully kissed her and said "Goodbye", and as we left the room she turned to Mother and said, "They won't miss me." Mother protested; but it was true.

CHAPTER SEVENTEEN

Echoes of India

THE GRANDPARENTS, Salmon and Fletcher, never met. They would have had nothing to say to each other. Mother and Father met and married in India without any concern for each other's background. They were captivated with each other; Father dashing in his military uniform, Mother gay and pretty, with a flair for clothes. She was living at Government House and helped the Governor's wife, Lady Porter, give garden parties to the army. It was all a far cry from a Suffolk farm and a London livery tailor's.

Mother had progressed to India via a series of happy coincidences. She was brought up in Suffolk with her four brothers at Dalton's Farm, Stoke-by-Nayland, where my Grandfather Fletcher was a tenant farmer for the Rowleys of Tendring Hall. The farm was some distance from the village and only reached by a long lane from the highroad, or by crossing several fields. Distance never deterred my indomitable grandmother, who visited any sick or lonely person needing attention at any time of the day or night.

She worked hard in her roomy farmhouse, scrubbing stone floors, collecting water from a pump in the yard and cooking on a black kitchen range, feeding and washing for her family of boys. But people told me when I was a child that she would set off alone at dusk, when her work was done, swinging her lantern, often walking several miles across rough land to make sure a sick cottager was comfortable for the night. She returned much later with no reassuring lights in cottage windows to guide her; even if it had not been open country, folk went to bed early and rose soon after dawn.

Mother went to Stoke village school, but she was quick and bright, reading and writing fluently, and clever with her needle. After school she was apprenticed to Lizzie Riddlestone for a while to learn dressmaking. The first job she ever mentioned to us was as a companion to an elderly woman living in Kent, the mother of the Rev. Horace Wilkinson, vicar of Stoke-by-Nayland. This must have been a rewarding relationship. Mother must have been a

Mother in a silk wedding gown and Father, dashing in his military uniform, after their wedding in India in 1910.

Mother and Father surrounded by members of his regiment and other guests, with Lady Porter sitting beside Mother.

very young woman, but she remembered that period with great pleasure. Mother absorbed atmosphere, speech and habits like a sponge, and old Mrs Wilkinson gained a young and lively companion who would happily change from renovating clothes to making sweets with her in the kitchen or accompanying her on visits to the grand houses in the neighbourhood. The most important of these was Knole, the home of the Sackville-Wests; the coachman drove them there to visit, or just to leave the inevitable visiting card.

This experience led to her only other and much more important job. Lady Porter, then Mrs Leslie Porter, a friend of the Rowleys, heard of her success with Mrs Wilkinson and asked her if she would go to India with her. Her husband was, I think, Governor of the United Provinces. Mother always spoke of herself as a companion, but I suspect she was really engaged as a lady's maid. It was another happy relationship; Lady Porter became my sister's godmother, and the Rev. Horace Wilkinson's daughter, Mrs Luttman, became mine. It was a wonderful opportunity for Mother to escape from a warm but narrow village life, and a very daring step for her to take.

She nearly died from seasickness on the voyage out; she was probably petrified with fear of the sea. When she returned home in 1910 with my father on their honeymoon trip she was equally terrified. He spent his days walking smartly round the deck while she lay at death's door in their cabin. She was so ill that the ship's doctor insisted on removing her from the ship at Marseilles to continue her journey overland. That was her last venture abroad.

Once in India she blossomed. It was never too hot for her. She loved the glamour of Government House. Her bearer was devoted to her, and she was as happy satisfying her curiosity about his family as going on safaris into the jungle or helping Lady Porter organise functions.

Ruth and I were properly impressed when she told us that her bearer slept outside her door to protect her, and that he begged her to time her visits to his family carefully because his wife, a strict Hindu, would throw away the meal she had prepared if Mother's Christian shadow fell across it. We learned, too, that she had ridden on an elephant which used its trunk to help her to mount or to pick a flower for her.

Photographs of their wedding reception given to them by the Porters, were splendid and fascinating to us children. Father, surrounded by his regiment, was resplendent in dark dress uniform with much gold braid, clutching his white topee across his middle; and Mother was tiny, with a huge bouquet, yards of tulle veiling and a long flounced silk gown and train. This dress was sentimentally preserved for future generations, wrapped in a sheet in a special trunk, along with Grandma's long embroidered and beribboned cotton knickers. They were all splendid additions to my children's dressing-up box in the sober aftermath of the Second World War.

Mother's waist was nineteen inches, while mine was depressingly plump; even my two daughters found the gown tight. I made the tulle veil into the skirts of party frocks for them, but my efforts ended miserably. They came home with limp remnants hanging from the waist; the material had rotted and tore to pieces when they were chased and caught.

Faint echoes of India haunted our country childhood. Father's topee hung incongruously on the back of the scullery door, and on a really hot day he would change into a shantung suit and lounge in a deckchair in the garden, where a gaily-coloured woven cotton hammock hung between two fruit trees. Mother had brought back many brass bowls and ornaments, and a large tray, most of them tourists' souvenirs from the Benares Bazaar. She cleaned them regularly with a messy lemon and silver sand; no ordinary Brasso was good enough to penetrate the intricate designs of queer animals, vegetation and Hindu gods. Her beautiful Indian hand-embroidered cotton and muslin cloths were brought out only for visitors.

My parents sprinkled their conversation with odd Hindi words: they always had *chota hazri* in the early morning; tea was always *char*. Lots of things were *pukka*; and we swallowed snippets of information about Lucknow, Benares, Poona and the trek to the hill stations in the rainy season when the plains below looked as if the lid had been taken off the copper.

We spent hours poring over their many shiny brown photographs of the Durbars of Indian princes they had attended, of the Fort at Agra, of Father's rigidly smart polo team, and of Mother leaning on a balcony in a large hat and flowing dress carrying the familiar sunshade. We handled a lovely mother-of-pearl model of the Taj Mahal, until one of its turrets finally snapped off.

Father occasionally talked of the Ghurkas, for whom he had a great admiration, and we glimpsed a more serious life on the North-West Frontier. They mentioned the poverty of Calcutta, but their attitude was entirely paternalistic: it was a white man's world, and they were helping the Indians to acquire Western culture, and showing a benevolent interest in their way of life. To us now, with our concern for the developing world and our appreciation of other, older cultures, this feeling of Empire seems incredible; yet they were understanding, caring people.

We turned the photographs over and romanced with them on winter evenings, marvelling how far they had come down to earth in a country village. But Mother and Father were happy there in the house by the wood, draughty and inconvenient as it was. The wood was friendly and sheltering, sometimes gay with the chatter of birds, at other times calm with the stillness of night.

Young Indian princes preparing to rehearse their part in the Delhi Durbar.

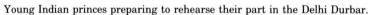

CHAPTER EIGHTEEN

Train to School

MOTHER was incorrigibly cheerful first thing in the morning. She woke us with a song and a can of hot water; we groaned and failed to appreciate such gaiety so early. She tipped the cold water out of the wash-stand jug into the bowl, and if we were too lazy to move she added the hot water so that we had to hurry before it cooled. In winter this was only a matter of minutes, as there was often a layer of ice on the water in the jug. We had to dress and undress by candlelight, too, and reading in bed was with a torch when candles were forbidden for fear of fire.

In 1924 Ruth and I started school at the Herts and Essex High School for Girls in Bishop's Stortford. In those days it had a junior school and a small boarding school next door, so many of the children were fee-paying. In fact, scholarship children were known to be bright but poor. My parents had wrestled for some months with the problem of where to send Ruth. I had a county scholarship, but Ruth was nearly thirteen and Father would have to pay for her, for they were determined that she should have a comparable education. The problem was to find a school where she would be happy and not overshadowed by me. Ruth was kind and generous and showed no signs of jealousy, but she had no interest or ability in school work. They considered the girls' convent school in Bishop's Stortford, in spite of Mother's apprehension of possible contamination from Roman Catholicism, but finally decided to send her to the school I was to attend. With hindsight and our knowledge of psychology one might doubt their wisdom; Ruth was always two classes below me, and I invariably did her homework for her, but on the other hand we were very close and to have been separated at that time might have been quite traumatic for her. We had a very happy and supportive relationship, and I like to think that I gave her confidence.

By 7.30 am we had to set off on our bicycles on the three-and-a-half-mile ride to Harlow station to catch the 8.28 train to Bishop's Stortford. Fog was the worst hazard; with no street lights and no pavements country roads were difficult to negotiate. Fortunately when the fog was really thick the train was always late, sometimes as much as two hours. Many schoolchildren were catching the train, so station officials usually took pity on us stamping up and down the platform and lit a good fire in the waiting room. If they failed to do this we crossed the line to the "up" platform and took possession of the roaring coal fire in the waiting room there. Businessmen waiting for the London train were always coddled, but they did not really appreciate our clumsy intrusion.

Mother had definite ideas on gear for wet weather. She insisted on swathing us in raincoats, mackintosh capes, sou'westers and hateful leggings with cords and two rows of hooks down the side. They were hideous, and difficult to wrench undone when the train was signalled and our hands were cold. The station cycle-shed was on the "up" side, so we had to work quickly. Fortunately the porters had no scruples about children dashing across the lines behind the train just in time to leap on before it pulled away.

If it was a really wet day at school, music was provided during break for ballroom dancing in the hall or gym. Bosoms clamped together, we one-stepped or foxtrotted around the room, earnestly pump-handling. In the stage version of *The Prime of Miss Jean Brodie* the scene where girls in gym-slips danced together was hilariously reminiscent of these days.

By special permission from the headmistress, Miss Hammill, Ruth and I were allowed to wear brown overcoats instead of the regulation navy blue, simply because Mother had made them for us and could not afford to replace them until they were worn out. Those coats caused us miserable discomfort: teachers on duty in

Herts and Essex High School, 1924. I am on the right of the back row, Ruth sixth from right in the middle row, with Miss Granville-Smith, our teacher, in the centre.

Ruth and me in our
school clothes.

the cloakroom pounced on us to demand the reason why we were
not wearing the correct dress, and girls commented on special
favours. We hated being different.

The routine of journeys to school was broken only once. The
General Strike in 1926 left us stranded. We were the only children
from Matching going out of the village to school. For a few days we
plodded on our cycles to Bishop's Stortford, using the backroads
through Sheering, Hatfield Heath and Little Hallingbury, a
journey of more than twelve miles. We enjoyed it as a novelty, so
long as the weather was fine and no-one expected us to do more
than sit back and relax at school. We had to avoid one energetic
games mistress, liable to turn us out to career up and down the
hockey pitch. I never was any good at running.

After several days organisation took over. The few cars in the
village were mustered to transport us by rota, and we were
delighted to be swept to school in our Guide Captain's Renault and
collected again at night, to the admiration of our pedestrian
friends.

On our usual return journey the only convenient train left at 3.20, so afternoon lessons were amazingly short. However, out-of-school activities such as music and drama meant staying on till a later train, and a dreary uphill ride from the station in the dark. We had no fears, but Father was anxious and often cycled to meet us. Occasionally I had to stay really late and then a bed was found for me in the boarding house, which was ruled by Miss Bentley, a tall mannishly-dressed woman whose smart, straight-laced looks belied her true nature: she was kind and welcoming.

At home Mother's housework for the morning was minutely programmed. Before we had arrived down to breakfast she had always swept the stairs down with a brush and dustpan, polishing the brass stair-rods and clipping them back in place if it was the right day. As soon as we had left for school she tackled the main chores with her usual vigour. Feather beds had to be shaken from each corner in turn, bedroom rugs were rolled up and hurled out of the bedroom windows into the garden, ready to be shaken. It was a pity that they couldn't be hurled up again. Slops were emptied into a china pail and carried off to the chicken run to throw over the nettles.

When it was spring-cleaning time we were in misery for weeks. Mother was impossibly thorough. Every carpet, rug, or strip of coconut matting was heaved out on to the lawn and beaten soundly. Floors were scrubbed with buckets of hot water heated laboriously on the kitchener in heavy iron saucepans. Everything washable was put into the copper, and Father was reluctantly inveigled into decorating.

His chief hate was paper-hanging. Clad in old flannelette pyjamas and a soft tweed hat, he took up his brush and paste. Mother readily offered help and advice, but was finally beaten into retreat because he became increasingly impatient as wall followed wall. He had to cope with columns of pasted paper by himself, and became thoroughly irritable as he dabbed it on himself and on everything around. We were all generous in our praise for the final result, but it took Father days to recover. He consoled himself in the garden, and Mother fervently polished everything in sight. None of us was comfortable until the fever was over.

We could not afford regular help in the house. Mother had a young nursemaid, Katie, to help sometimes when we were little, and Mrs Seymour came in occasionally when Mother was old and crippled with arthritis; but people were always ready to help. After my father's death, paths were miraculously swept clear of snow before she got up in the morning, and pails of water were filled at the tap and put on the doorstep. Village people shared a concern for each other; they had lived together for a long time.

In our first years at the High School Ruth and I corresponded for a while with two boys from Newport Grammar School—an oddly-matched pair from Sheering who caught the same train as us, although we were much too timid to talk to them on the train. Like us they rode to the station on their bicycles, and sometimes we exchanged a few words in the evening, leaning on our bicycles where our roads diverged. My sister, of course, wrote to the tall handsome boy; I was left with his short, freckled, sandy-haired companion, who aroused not a flicker of passion in me. It was all quite harmless and fizzled out for want of enthusiasm, and as a result of a greater preoccupation with school work.

Ruth was pretty and attractive to boys; I was plain and talkative. The boys were wary of me and my devastating remarks. When we were out together the boys always wanted to kiss her, but she was usually madly coy, so I impatiently offered to stand in for her in order to bring the whole boring business to an end. My offers were spurned.

The only boy we were allowed to play with regularly was Mr

The Herts and Essex High School at Bishop's Stortford, where Ruth and I were pupils from 1924 to 1931.

93

Walls' grandson, Owen, a plump youth with heavy hornrimmed glasses, a splendid singing voice, and an inability to rush around and share in our more energetic pastimes. Friends asked him out to tea with us, unaware that he was at the stage of being preoccupied with female bottoms, and if we were left alone in the hay, sucking stalks and chatting desultorily, he was known to ask us to take our knickers down. We were obliging, and he was curious and had no sisters.

We were all incredibly innocent. Mother would have been frightened if she had known; Grandma Fletcher would have assigned us straight to Hell. We didn't think it was worth mentioning.

Marriage Feast Room — Matching Ch

CHAPTER NINETEEN

A New and Exciting World

THE YEAR in which I celebrated my tenth birthday, 1923, opened a door into a wonderful new world. The years from then until 1931 which I spent at the High School had an overwhelming influence on me. It was like walking through a door to a new country, vast and limitless, offering endless possibilities, new interests and books galore.

I was a country child, steeped in my surroundings, and limited by them; protected and loved by my family, and longing to spread my wings. Music was what I heard in church or could play myself. We had no radio at first, and never a gramophone or record-player. Books were bought only as birthday presents or for Christmas. I had read everything at home from *Pet Marjorie*, *Grimm's Fairy Tales* and all L. M. Allcott's books to those on the adults' bookshelves, including most of Dickens and the novels of Rosa Nouchette Carey, of which I can only remember one title, *Rue with a Difference*.

The Essex County Library sent a van to the village at intervals of several months, when Father and the headmistress who had succeeded Mr Gibbins spent an afternoon choosing several dozen books to put on the shelves in the back room of the Institute Hall for anyone to borrow. Father made sure that there were plenty of history, travel and biography for himself, and romantic novels for Mother. I swallowed them all. I read quite unselectively all the books of Zane Grey, Jerome K. Jerome, Wilkie Collins, Edgar Wallace, Gene Stratton Porter and Florence Barclay, whose books I still remember as a curious mixture of sentimentality and religion.

Then came the High School. I met poetry—and prose which had the music and cadences of poetry; and words in all sorts of combinations and groups, describing things I knew and loved so that they took on a magic and beauty which moved and excited me. I learned so much by heart. This is still with me; a source of wonder and a comfort for ever.

It is probably not fashionable to enjoy Tennyson now, but I shall never forget the Gardener's daughter "with hair more black than ashbuds in the front of March", or the Dying Swan on the river where

> Ever the weary wind went on
> And took the reed tops as it went.

Adolescence coincided with discovering Wordsworth and Coleridge, Keats and Shelley and Matthew Arnold. It would be impossible to describe the excitement that I felt when I first read Keats' *Endymion*, his Odes, Shelley's *West Wind* and Matthew Arnold's *Scholar Gipsy* and *Thyrsis*. All the common trees and flowers I knew so well took on a special radiance when they described them. Their use of words and the feelings they evoked were to me overwhelming. I was sorry for anyone who had not discovered these poets; I was grateful that I had been privileged to meet them. I might have missed them.

I found it almost unbearable then to read their poetry aloud in class. So much so that after School Certificate, when it was taken for granted that I would go to Cambridge to do a Tripos when I left school, women not being awarded degrees then, I insisted that I would do it in History and not in English. I never explained that the thought of reading poetry aloud at University, where men might listen, frightened me to death. I was equally good at history, so it was accepted, and I finally did Higher School Certificate with History and French as main and English and Latin as subsidiary subjects. This all goes to prove, of course, that I was immature and shy with strange men, who were unknown quantities to me.

I had always been treated by my father like a boy. He often called me "Nance, old boy!" I expect he was disappointed that his second child was not a boy.

Studying history opened more doors. Miss Gaynor Lewis, Welsh and a fervent disciple of Lloyd George, was the best teacher I have known, then or since. She had not long come down from Oxford and was full of enthusiasm; I was hooked from the beginning. She made every period of history interesting and alive, peopled with characters we felt we should have recognised if we had met them in the street: Gustavus Adolphus, Palmerston, Disraeli, Napoleon, Bismarck. It was a fascinating and rich tapestry.

She had, too, an utterly logical and organised mind. When discussing national events or world movements she saw the causes and effects in clear headings and sub-headings, all neatly listed in her mind. We could see them, too. Consequently she unwittingly taught us an invaluable lesson in making clear and concise notes in tabulated form as we later listened to lectures; and in selecting and organising points for arguments in a straightforward, logical sequence. I have always felt grateful to her.

96

She was fun, too, with her passionate allegiance to Lloyd George and her energetic careering up and down the pitch in the staff hockey team. She introduced me to the League of Nations Union, when I joined her junior branch at school. It was the beginning of a lasting interest for me. Later I joined the Cambridge University branch; and when I was teaching, I formed my own junior branch. Since the Second World War I have worked for many years on UNA committees.

Miss Hammill, a quiet, cultured headmistress, somewhat aloof, also opened other doors wide for me, particularly when I reached the sixth form. She taught us no fixed subject, but often came to talk to us of her special interest, the Italian Renaissance, introducing us to a wealth of paintings and sculptures. She loved them passionately and chose reproductions to hang on classroom walls. Fra Lippo Lippi's *Annunciation* hung behind my head. We were an appreciative audience, fewer than twenty of us, and we learned to understand something of the artist's skills and vision when we studied a great painting, and to recognise the works of Leonardo da Vinci, Giotto, Botticelli and Michaelangelo. We visited the great Italian Art Exhibition at the Royal Academy, in 1930 I think, and we were able to feel something of the exultation great art evokes. I remember *The Birth of Venus* hanging alone on an end wall; the figure seemed on the point of stepping out to meet us.

Miss Hammill arrived in the classroom always accompanied by her dog, Barney, who curled up in the kneehole cavity of her desk while she talked. One term she gave us a short course in simple logic, drawing figures to illustrate it graphically; I cannot remember them, but it was an enjoyable exercise. She might have been a feminist in advance of her time, because she frequently used such premises as "All men are liars", with a faint smile but no comment. Such topics were not discussed in classrooms then.

Drama and Music clubs were out-of-school activities, so they meant catching the later train home. Since it was an all-girls' school, and I was neither slim nor pretty, I was always cast as a man in school productions; I played Sir Oliver Surface in *The School for Scandal*.

Visits to the theatre in London were not very frequent, but my parents found the money for me to join school parties. It was an exciting world in which the plays of Shakespeare became a rich experience. We visited the Lyric and The Old Vic, where John Gielgud was a rising star. I first saw him as a singularly restless Hotspur, and later as a dramatic King Lear. I bought a pin-up photograph of him to take home. It was oddly dated; he wore a large-brimmed trilby hat, perched rakishly on the side of his head, like a good-looking gangster. I kept him on my dressing-table for

97

years. I was enchanted by young Robert Helpmann, too; he was the most charming Feste I have ever seen, and *Twelfth Night* is a favourite play of mine. His pin-up picture stood beside John Gielgud's.

I can remember going to the cinema only twice in all my schooldays. That was to see Charlie Chaplin after school in Bishop's Stortford. Mother was not quite sure that films were fit entertainment, and we were not bothered; there was no money to spare, distances were too great, and we were much too busy in the country. The film stars were hardly even names to me; I was amazed to meet girls at college who lived in towns and had been going to the cinema regularly twice a week.

The music staff at the High School, Miss Wood and Miss Kingdon, were very helpful to me, perhaps because I was a pupil of Dora Brinkworth, a former student of theirs. They sometimes asked me to play accompaniments at school concerts, and I joined their Music Club, where they taught me to listen to music with a critical ear. It was the beginning of "canned" music, and they were very wary of it.

I was taking Associated Board music examinations throughout these schooldays, and every Saturday morning cycled to Matching vicarage for my music lesson. As the exams became more difficult it was necessary to practise two hours a day, but this became impossible after School Certificate and during my two years in the sixth form; finally piano lessons had to go. I was reluctant to give up because I had only just discovered the delights of playing Beethoven, Mozart or Haydn sonatas, and because I listened to so little music that I needed help in interpretation and a boost to my confidence.

I loved jazz, too. Ruth and I arrived home from school most afternoons in time to hear Jack Payne, and later Henry Hall, conduct their bands in a programme of dance music. It was a highlight in our day. We danced together, up and down in a small space beside the dining table, I being the man propelling Ruth around. This was, of course, after we had been given a friend's cast-off loudspeaker set; before that we had to fiddle with a cat's whisker, an exercise guaranteed to reduce Father to frustrated impatience.

I spent many odd hours playing jazz on the piano. I felt more confident than I did with the classics that my interpretation was good enough. The Doll Dance was my speciality. I also went through a pretentious and dreary period of singing and accompanying myself in popular songs. These efforts should have been squashed at the outset. I became ridiculous, and blush to think that I once put on a long evening dress to entertain the Women's Institute at an afternoon meeting.

My class at the Herts and Essex High School. I am in the front row, second from the right.

In the summer of 1931 I was eighteen and my time at the High School was coming to an end. What was I going to do? I thought it might be fun to go on the stage, or train as a secretary to an MP, or go to China as a missionary. These were all treated as frivolous suggestions and not encouraged. My parents were convinced that I must take up teaching; it would be a secure job. It was now the Thirties, a period which still conjures up visions of appalling unemployment. Security was essential for all young people then: security in a job; security in marriage. No-one offered me conflicting advice, and I knew that I should enjoy teaching. Above all it would give me the immediate advantage of prolonging my academic studies, and I was a voracious student. I had only one reservation: I must go to Cambridge. So I agreed to apply to Homerton College for a Teachers' Training Course.

99

However, when Higher Certificate results came out Miss Hammill sent for me and insisted that I should try for Girton to read for an Arts degree. She assured me that she could get me a County Major Scholarship to help with fees. My hopes began to soar as she sent for my father.

He arrived after school one afternoon, when only Miss Hammill and I remained in the building. I watched him enter the gate and come up the path from the sixth form window, where I stood for the next half an hour hugging the hot-water pipes while he was closeted in Miss Hammill's study. I watched him leave with a measured step, head on one side, looking at the ground. After a while the door opened and Miss Hammill came and stood quietly beside me.

At last she said, "What a nice man! I wish all my fathers were as nice. He can't do it you know, Nancie. We've gone through it thoroughly. There's no way he can find the money; even with a scholarship. . . I'm sorry."

I had expected it. I think I had already accepted it. I just reiterated that I would go to Cambridge.

In those days all the staff at Herts and Essex were Oxbridge graduates. All pupils were sent to Oxford or to Cambridge. I can remember only one exception, who went to London. There was never any suggestion that it might be less expensive to go to other universities; there were no alternatives.

I was not unduly depressed. A university education in those days, particularly for women, was rare; there was no tradition of it in our family; and the only man in our village who was at Cambridge was Henry Harding-Jones, our rich landlord's son, who later became chairman of the Gas Board. I didn't aspire to his heights. Only one other child from Matching had gained a scholarship to the High School during my school life. Our expectations were very modest.

I had no yardstick to measure what I was missing. I was told that Essex would give me a hundred per cent loan for two years to go to a Training College; I would have to work for them on qualifying, and the grant would be paid back by docking instalments at source from my monthly cheque. I thought this a fair arrangement, and my parents were spared great sacrifices.

On my return from school that evening Father said how understanding Miss Hammill had been, and apologised to me for my having to turn down a County Scholarship. His income was impossibly low. I understood; but he rather spoilt the effect by adding in all seriousness, "If you'd been a boy, perhaps we might have managed it somehow; but after a few years you'll marry, and it would all be wasted."

There was no acceptable reply.

CHAPTER TWENTY

Last Summer at Home

THAT SUMMER at home was a bridge; Cambridge waited on the other side. I was excited at the prospect of leaving home, but was making sure that I savoured the last of my freedom to loiter and visit, to fritter my time, to collect together material things to remind me of home, and to find the encouragement I needed. Father was a great believer in stiff upper lips and no fuss: it mattered not at all if I brought home a glowing school report, repeating several "Excellents", his highest commendation was "Not bad". We understood each other perfectly.

Ruth had already left home; she left school four years before me. For a year or two she worked at Harlow College as an assistant secretary, and then went away to become assistant matron at a children's home in Billericay, and later at a similar home in Tiptree. Our close days were over; we drifted further and further apart as we went our different ways, pursuing different interests, always pleased to see each other, but at longer and longer intervals, and with only our common background to share now.

Mother worried when Ruth wrote home of men friends, and finally asked me to go and see her specifically to warn her against a fate worse than death. I reluctantly agreed. Transport was always a problem when the journey was crosscountry, but by catching a series of buses I arrived at Billericay. I'm afraid our conversation was not very serious; Ruth could look after herself. I realise now that she might have been desperately lonely; we had no phone, nor a car, and she hated writing letters. I take comfort in the fact that Mother was a marvellous letter writer, racily keeping us posted with all the news. Father only occasionally penned a short, laconic note.

I gave a farewell tennis party to all my friends at school on our bumpy shared court by the wood. We made plans to meet again, but only four of us kept in irregular contact. Joan was going to Girton; another girl, Ruth, was already there; and Lorna was going up to Oxford. We met for a weekend's camping at Thaxted. We walked a little, but talked interminably, sitting outside our tent. We were deadly serious, full of high ideals and high-falutin' nonsense, putting the world to rights and agreed in our determination not to "prostitute our art by taking up journalism". We felt the world would unfold before us, full of opportunities, and awaiting our earnest contributions. Perhaps it was just as well that I had to cut short my weekend and return home with a painful boil in my ear. Mother's remedy was to tuck a spring onion in it, and miraculously it worked, although it did not prevent me from having a miserable succession of them.

As an antidote to intellectual activities, I wallowed in *The Tatler* and *Country Life*. Mrs Harding-Jones dumped a pile of recent copies on Mother from time to time; Mother looked for familiar names, while I learned to recognise all the moneyed aristocracy at their various pursuits. I was quite bothered for some time by A. N. Other. He seemed to turn up in various guises on all sorts of occasions. I decided he must be hiding his identity because he was in a compromising situation. I finally unravelled it, but still fail to understand why such an extraordinarily contrived title should be assumed. My husband tells me that it was also used on Rugby lists pinned on his school notice board when the captain had not yet decided on a player.

Ruth, on the left, as assistant matron of a children's home in Tiptree, Essex.

Faggoters Farmhouse, the home of Mr and Mrs Parsons.

It was fortunate for me that I came to know a family who had come to live at Faggoters, a farmhouse between Housham Tye and High Laver. The father, a very tall elderly man with a drooping moustache, Mr Parsons, was a director of Odham's Press. He loved books and was always interesting to me. He occasionally gave me books, and in return I often accompanied him on the piano when he was well over seventy and felt moved to sing a wheezy *Because*. His wife had to fetch him from North Weald station every evening in their car. It was a hazardous journey because she had only started driving when she was over sixty, tests were not yet introduced, and she never did learn to reverse; so she had to charm any driver meeting her in a narrow lane to move his vehicle back. Fortunately traffic was usually light. During the summer I often accompanied her to give her moral support. On the return journey we invariably stopped at *The Talbot*, North Weald, and while he had his whisky I was treated to a hot peppermint.

Their two sons owned the garage, "Parsons and Parsons", on the A11 at Potter Street, opposite the *Sun and Whalebone*. They were both rather dashing. Harold, the elder, loved speed and had been known to ditch his car round sharp corners on his way home; but I loved to be driven in his sleek Talbot Tourer to Cambridge and back at some speed in the evening, or to Hoddesdon to the

103

cinema. Lou, his brother, confined his speed trails to T.T. racing in the Isle of Man.

Until the last two years I had been appallingly ignorant of politics and current affairs. Mother did not encourage me to read the newspapers because they contained too many murders and too many seamy stories, and my parents never bought a quality newspaper. Father persuaded himself that he always saw both sides of the question by taking a *Daily Mail* and a *News Chronicle*, but he believed only the *Mail* and remained a determined Tory. When I came home from college with strange Socialist leanings he refused to argue, and hoped that I would grow out of such heresies.

Mr Salmon from Matching Green, no relation to us, delivered newspapers each day on a bicycle after collecting them from Harlow. On Sundays another man on a bicycle arrived on the Tye about lunchtime. Sunday papers were frowned on: Mother was adamant that they were not to be read, but Father managed to slip out for one on occasions. Perhaps it was good that we were well occupied on Sundays going to church and chapel, because we were not allowed to play games, to sew or knit, and we could read only improving or informative books. I read the eight volumes of *The Children's Encyclopedia* from cover to cover, and amassed a positive rag-bag of unconnected snippets of information, before I was able to claim that homework had to be done and thus insist on reading my English and French set books.

Mother and Father at Dover-court, where they would enjoy a holiday each year.

Dovercourt Bay before the Second World War, with the covered pavilion in the background where Mother and Father would listen to the orchestra.

Even Mother was shaken two years later when the father of a Swedish friend of mine was staying for the weekend and, asked what he would like to do on Sunday afternoon, replied that he would like to play a little clock golf. Her convictions deserted her; we all played clock golf. Her mother's daughter she might have been, but Grandma Fletcher would not have given in; she would have launched into a reproving sermon. Mother's permissive society was beginning.

For a few years Suffolk holidays had come to an end. My grandparents and Frank Welham were dead. Emmie had moved into The Laurels with her farmer husband and three young children. The holidays revived again later when my four children were young too, and we were welcomed with open arms, however littered and noisy the house became. Emmie rivalled her mother's cooking, and the boys loved to help on the early-morning milk round.

Now Father and Mother spent a quiet week in apartments at

105

Dovercourt Bay each year. They bought season tickets for the orchestra which played every day in the covered seafront pavilion and thoroughly enjoyed a lazy holiday. This year I went with them for the last time. I can remember feeling not entirely happy, just reading and walking: I felt frustrated at the slow pace and lack of young, stimulating company. I think they sensed this and were hurt. Mother protested, "We're too old for you, dear." I felt depressed and ungrateful. It was time to move on.

I had had to apply to five Training Colleges on my application form, arranged in order of preference from Homerton at the top and Goldsmiths' second, down to Furzedown. All but Homerton wrote back immediately and offered me a place without an interview; Homerton asked me to an interview in London.

The Principal, Miss M. M. Allen, luckily accepted me, but not before I had been asked to take off my hat, and had lied in response to her demand why I had not taken English instead of History as a main subject when I had gained a distinction in it. Then, as I went out of room, she demanded brusquely how tall I was. I carelessly replied, "Five-foot-two," and she firmly corrected me "Five *feet* two, Miss Salmon."

I felt I had not made a very good impression. Miss Allen was a large and intimidating woman, with a strong Scottish accent and a determination to enunciate every word distinctly, with much guttural sound and many twisting lip movements. I was wary of her; but later, when I got to know her well, I liked and respected her greatly.

Mother's preparations were more extensive than mine. She went to London and bought materials, then spent hours at the dining-room table cutting out and sewing on her old Singer hand machine, making all new clothes for me, from silk pyjamas to evening frocks. I was going to look as well dressed as anyone else while she could use a needle. Since I had lived in gym tunics and navy blue skirts and blouses, all teamed with hideous black woollen stockings, for the last eight years, I was delighted. We had to buy a trunk to put them all in.

It was the end of summer. I played a lot of tennis, went for long walks over the fields, and strolled through the wood. I pottered in the garden helping to pick apples, and followed Mother around the house doing chores. I was helping her with the ritual bedmaking on the day before I left, when she asked me to kneel beside her. She spoke aloud a very simple prayer, earnestly committing me to God's help and care. Her religion was part of her, utterly sincere, and I tried not to be embarrassed. But I determined to be anonymous next term and not to join any special church. I was beginning to feel suffocated by other people's beliefs, and wanted space to sort out my own convictions.

CHAPTER TWENTY-ONE

Cambridge Terms

WITH the trunk stowed in the luggage van, I boarded the train at Bishop's Stortford for Cambridge. Several Homertonians were already on the train and made themselves known to me. We all had trunks, so, although the college was within walking distance up Hills Road, it was imperative for us to hire a taxi, an extravagant luxury.

Mr Cousins, the head porter, supervised the unloading in the college entrance, aided by his son, known as "Ask-me-Dad", also in a green baize apron. "Ask-me-Dad" was apparently incapable of taking any decision without referring to parental authority. There were no lifts, so they tramped up hundreds of stone steps with those bulky trunks. Mine remained in my small room as extra seating, covered with a piece of flowered cretonne which Mother had thoughtfully provided.

My first room overlooked the kitchens and maids' bedrooms, so that there was a constant stream of returning footsteps after ten o'clock, and much disjointed singing all day long of *Goodnight Sweetheart*, the current popular song. The room was not very comfortable, but adequate, and I was uncritical. There was a tradition that every student on leaving donated one pound of her first salary to a fund used to provide extra furnishings for students' rooms. They must have been very basic originally; we all went to Woolworths and fitted up our own reading lamps.

When I visited Ruth and Joan at Girton I was envious of their two rooms each, carpeted, with open coal fires and with facilities for making tea in their rooms. We were not allowed to eat or have any outside visitors in our rooms—much too dangerous in bed-sitting rooms; and visitors from home had to be entertained in a formal sitting room on the ground floor.

Homerton had been built as a men's college, and it followed the pattern of all Cambridge colleges, with kitchens opposite a huge dining hall with long tables and an impressive procession of waiters or waitresses as each course was served. We had no choice of menu, but the food, augmented with Mother's cake, was adequate.

The staff sat "on high", disappointingly old and grey, I felt on that first evening; but Miss Allen made an imposing entrance in a

Students at Homerton College on May Day, 1933, with me seated second from the right. At far left of the same row is Dora Shafe, better known today as the author, Miss Reade.

long black lace gown. After supper she welcomed us, and next morning called all the First Year together to hear her famous speech on the Five Thousand. We had been warned to expect this: there were five thousand young men in Cambridge, and we were reminded that impeccable behaviour was expected of us. The paternalistic society was keeping up with us; this was going to be an extended sixth form. We had to have exeats to be out of college after ten o'clock, and we had to enter in a book the name and college of any man we were visiting.

I was disappointed to find that many students had no higher qualifications than School Certificate, so that the academic syllabi were really geared to a sixth-form level. Particularly in History I found that I was repeating all the work I had done for Higher School Certificate. This could have been just boring repetition, but because the mass of written work was easily within my grasp I was able to find time for many extra activities.

I wrote a history thesis, a psychology thesis, a book of child study, and short papers to read to the English and History Societies. I had time to read; there were so many gaps to fill. I read Shaw, Arnold Bennett and found *Clayhanger* very amusing; modern poets like Francis Thompson; and the First World War poets, including Rupert Brooke. I thought his *Great Lover* was tremendously exciting; I appreciated "the benison of hot water", "the cool kindliness of sheets"; I was not quite sure of the "rough male kiss of blankets", but it sounded thrilling.

I continued French as an extra, and acted in regular Saturday evening one-act plays. This meant rehearsing before breakfast during the week before—not my favourite pastime.

The subject which brought a new dimension into my life at this time was psychology, including the theory and practice of education. Dr Waterhouse, lecturer in psychology, stood out with distinction from among her fellow lecturers. I found her immensely stimulating, if rather intimidating. She looked like a slim elderly man with her grey hair closely shingled and her rather shuffling gait. She was extremely odd at times in her behaviour, and older students swore that she danced round lamp posts at full moon.

She did not suffer fools gladly, and treated with withering scorn a foolish comment in a seminar; but her lectures were erudite and probing, and she encouraged any real interest in the working of

Homerton College, Cambridge, is one of the best-known of Britain's teacher training colleges.

the mind. She had been in education a long time and when she spoke of deprivation in children, we felt she cared. She opened my horrified eyes to the sexual abuse of young children within the family in some slum areas. I was able to join a small group to study Plato's *Republic* with her, and found her very patient and illuminating.

May Day was a pagan revival at Homerton. I never quite came to terms with it. On the last day of April we were expected to trail out into the countryside and come back laden with greenery, even branches from trees, to decorate the stairways and public spaces. Then, on the day itself, we all wore white and had our photographs taken in year groups on the lawn. It seemed a complete anachronism to me, but everyone seemed to go along

King's College Chapel, Cambridge.

St John's College, Cambridge, where I sometimes attended services in the chapel.

with it as an almost sacred ritual, which was strange under a strictly religious Principal.

We were invited to join all the Cambridge University Societies, so I became a member of the League of Nations Union branch and later of an Anti-War Society, run by a very earnest group of young men. I felt very strongly about the cause until at one meeting they were discussing what should happen in the event of war: we must all immediately stand firm against war; we would naturally lose our jobs and be put in prison. They were so confident in their belief. I was horrified: my commitment went nowhere near such drastic acts; they were asking the impossible of me. I would not be able to give up my job; I could not let my parents down. They had banked on my security. I decided that I was no revolutionary.

Yet I understood and shared the feeling in the Thirties that Russia was conducting a fascinating experiment, and had achieved a miracle in educating so quickly an almost illiterate population. If this was socialism, it was obviously better for the majority than the Tsarist régime and crushing feudalism. We were idealists, and I can understand the genuine feelings which persuaded the Cambridge group of Maclean, Burgess, Philby and Blunt to opt for Communism. I cannot understand their treason, nor can I understand why, as they came to know the ruthless authoritarianism of the Communist Party, they remained under its spell. So many others with like views as students repudiated them later.

I had decided not to join a church group. There was quite a pressure to join one of the University church societies, with the added inducement that you would be asked to tea in private houses on Sunday afternoons, and would meet groups of undergraduates there. I was nearly seduced by the thought of a real fire to sit by just once in a while.

In spite of such temptations I remained free, and went to services at St John's College Chapel and at King's College Chapel. I loved the ritual and the music; and no-one shook me by the hand at the door and tried to persuade me to join in activities. A parson friend of mine said it was pure "soul culture" and nothing to do with Christianity, but for the time being it satisfied me.

The Cambridge Triennial Mission took place while I was up,

The Gate Tower at St John's College has St. John's statue placed above the entrance.

and this provided opportunities to be in the town in the evenings. I heard Dean Inge preach at Great St Mary's; not a particularly gloomy sermon, although I remember concentrating hard to follow him. His simple exhortation I remember, too: "Give what you know of yourself to what you know of God". There was an amazing service in the Round Church, which could hardly accommodate the crowd, who sat all over the steps and floor. They were inspiring meetings, a long way from the familiar chapel services at home.

Twice the Hon. Mrs Ernest Guinness sent out invitations to tea at the Garden House Hotel. A friend and I felt these must be accepted for the sake of a free tea, and to satisfy our curiosity about the Oxford Group, which was Mrs Guinness' special interest. She was a very sincere, warm person, and her psychology was brilliant. She talked about the group and the house parties which they organised in various parts of the country; and she produced Adonis-like undergraduates, in particular hefty rowing Blues, who made their public confessions with typical British understatement. I admired them enormously, particularly one tall blue-eyed young man with a devastating stutter who bravely made fun of it. I realised that I could never be persuaded to make similar confessions; not even for the sake of taking tea with glamorous men in comfortable surroundings.

The Greek play was, I think, a biennial Cambridge event. I knew not a word of Greek, but I had studied *Iphigenia in Aulis* and knew my Homer. Professor Gilbert Murray came up to college and gave a stunning lecture on Greek drama, and the actual performance was a very special occasion.

I had only one pound a month pocket money, so even then it would only stretch to a theatre or cinema visit if I cut out a Saturday afternoon tea in town. This was a pity, because entering a restaurant freely was entirely new to a country girl. We always walked into town, never spending a penny on bus fares, so that we could spend an hour having waffles and maple syrup at The Waffle; helping ourselves to a luscious slice of cake at The Copper Kettle; or dallying with a pot of tea at The Dorothy, where Percy and his orchestra played feet-tapping jazz. Percy was a Cambridge institution; very fat, good-humoured and silent, playing a grand piano with nonchalance and watching what was going on in the room at the same time. Once we were able to persuade the College authorities to engage Percy and his orchestra to play for an end of term ball at Homerton. I think they thought it was a little risky; but we loved it. I wonder what he thought of all of us, dressed in evening frocks, dancing with each other, with no young men in sight?

When we could afford it we joined the queue for the Gods

113

outside the Festival Theatre on a Saturday evening. I think Tyrone Guthrie was the director of it then. If the stalls were not full when the show was almost ready to begin he would walk along the queue and invite all of us students to fill up the stalls. I saw *Peer Gynt* and *1066 and All That* like this. The apron stage was so near the stalls that you felt you were part of the performance. They were magical evenings.

The New Theatre usually put on amateur performances, and I was once given tickets to see *Iolanthe* there. I had been introduced to Gilbert and Sullivan at school when Sir Arthur Cutforth had invited Joan Lightwood and me to dinner at his home in Sawbridgeworth and afterwards to London to a performance of *The Mikado* by the D'Oyly Carte Opera Company, as prizes in an essay competition. We giggled childishly at dinner, but loved the opera. *Iolanthe* was made rather more entertaining because undergraduates in the circle gently barracked the distinctly lumpy fairies when they danced across the stage.

There was so much to do and so much to hear. And public lectures were free. I heard Professor G. M. Trevelyan, whose books I had studied, Lord Wilton, the returned Viceroy of India, and I remember an amazing lecture on the White Slave Traffic, which was a complete revelation to me. Everyone else around looked so knowledgeable.

In the summer months we tumbled out of bed soon after dawn, leapt on our bicycles, raced down to Scudamore's boathouse and punted up the river for an hour before breakfast. It was all harmless fun; but we felt pretty daring. Punting up to Grantchester for a picnic on Sunday afternoons was a much more leisurely affair. We were noisy, excited groups, even desecrating the peace with our portable record players, most of us able to punt satisfactorily, but occasionally being a nuisance to swifter and more competent punters. Secretly I envied the languishing girl being punted romantically along by some young Greek god, deftly manipulating his pole and basking in her adoration. Romance still evaded me.

CHAPTER TWENTY-TWO

Farewell to Cambridge

M**Y FIRST** school practice was a disaster. I was training to teach senior pupils, but by some mishap I was sent to a junior school which was known to have "free discipline". This was a daunting prospect. I had to give a nature study lesson, which meant I had to learn all my facts because, lover of nature as I was, I was sadly lacking in knowledge of botany. I had learnt no such subject at the High School.

I spent the weekend cycling round the countryside collecting suitable specimens of twigs, enough for every child in the class. I gave my talk to rapt attention. All was well; I thought I was winning.

Then, in the accepted manner, the children were to examine the twigs and draw them. I gave them out feeling quite confident. They fought in the aisles for each other's twigs; no-one appeared satisfied that his was as good as his neighbour's. In such chaos I did a fair imitation of Father's parade-ground voice.

This was not appreciated by the regular class teacher, but it quelled the riot. I felt mortified. Miss Glennie, kind, elderly and lady-like, helped me plan my next lesson more circumspectly. It was to be on watersnails, about which I knew nothing. I practised drawing one; it appeared to have only one eye—perhaps it was a side view. I had to spend time before breakfast collecting specimens down by Fen Causeway. I hated it. I only wanted to teach English or history.

It finally dawned on the college staff that I was to teach seniors. My final school practice was at the Cambridge High School for Girls, where I had a lively, bright class of twelve-year-olds for history. I regained my confidence: I knew that this was what I wanted to do.

In 1933 I left with a First and a job waiting for me in Chingford, in a new Essex senior school for four hundred girls where I was to teach English and history to the top classes.

Cambridge proved difficult to leave. It had become a very special place; a conglomeration of moving and trivial sensations. Everywhere were grey college courts enclosing perfect lawns, quiet cloisters, panelled dining-rooms, candle-lit chapels with the unbelievably beautiful voices of the choristers rising to the vaulted roofs; narrow passageways and streets with dark bruised stone walls on either side; young men in dressing gowns, clutching towels, strolling across courts and along streets early in the morning in search of a bath. Bicycles were everywhere, with gowns and squares stuffed into the baskets in front until the evening, when proctors were vigilant to see that gowns were worn.

Rag Days came and went. Amusing tableaux held up traffic in the streets, with students collecting money disguised as road-menders or wearing ridiculous combinations of fancy dress. Only the most sober and respectably clad were allowed into Homerton to rattle their boxes, and they were discreetly supervised.

Linking New Court of St John's College to the older courts is the picturesque Bridge of Sighs, designed by Henry Hutchinson and built in 1831.

A contemplative atmosphere of learning was punctuated with shouts from punts and music from college rooms. More enduring were the glimpses of avenues of trees and lawns across the river and along the Backs, most attractive in the early spring with crocuses patterning the grass under the weeping willow trees. Behind them loomed the massive buildings of King's and Clare and the arched stone bridges, the sweep of gardens by St John's with its Bridge of Sighs, and, tucked away near the back entrance, the School of Pythagoras—evocative names. I was not to know that thirty years later my younger son, Peter, would be married in St John's Chapel and hold a reception on these same lawns. It would have been a flight of fancy then to think that he would be a Scholar and Wrangler, a Doctor of Theoretical Physics and a diplomat. Perhaps my dreams of Cambridge were fulfilled in him.

Queen's had a special fascination with its small ancient buildings and its wooden bridge; it had been Mr Brinkworth's college. Trinity Chapel housed memorials and plaques to the famous through the centuries, bringing history alive and our short dalliance with Cambridge into proportion. At Grantchester I was delighted to see that the church clock still stood at ten to three. The magnificence of King's College Chapel, with its delicate fan-vaulting and stained-glass windows in the chancel diffusing coloured light on a summer's day, was breathtaking. I was not convinced that it was built to the glory of God; rather it glorified the Tudor monarchy with its numerous Tudor roses and symbolic carving around the walls.

Only once did I return to Homerton for a reunion; not a satisfactory thing to do. Many of the staff were soon to retire, female society was too exclusive and as Dr Lawrence, then Chief Education Officer for Essex, once remarked in public, "Teachers are like manure: all right spread thinly, but dreadful in quantity!" Each year of students left en masse, and I would be quickly forgotten.

A few years later an extra teacher was needed at the school where I was teaching. The headmistress asked me to write to Homerton requesting them to recommend a student about to leave. I wrote to Dr Warehouse, introducing myself rather diffidently by suggesting that she might not remember me, but . . . Her reply began, "Of course, I remember you—a brilliant star in the firmament . . ." Could that have been me? No-one had ever suggested that that was a fitting metaphor. Had she muddled me with someone else? Perhaps with my friend and contemporary Dora Shafe, always clever and witty, who has since written prolifically as "Miss Read"?

I basked in the praise, and hoped it really did refer to me.

117

CHAPTER TWENTY-THREE

The Next Stage

THE TRUNK and I went back to Matching to a comfortable and lazy summer. The room Ruth and I had shared was now a boxroom and apple store. I had moved into the grandparents' room next door, looking out on the pond and the soft-fruit beds. Across the meadow the new row of council houses lined the road. The wood behind me was still full of bird-song. We still used oil lamps, too, and carried candles to light us to bed.

It was a strange, unsettled time. I was loath to leave for good, but travelling daily to Chingford would be impossible; and I needed a more challenging life. Matching was like a tree trunk at the centre of my life, adding growth rings around the perimeter at every stage; or perhaps a stone thrown into a pool with ever-increasing ripples slowly moving outwards until they merged into the whole.

I looked for digs in Chingford and found a modest room near the railway with a kind Cockney family who felt it was odd that I had no regular "young man". The craze to have a flat and do your own cooking was not then widespread. For twenty-five shillings a week I had full board, exclusive of weekends, when I usually went home. That cost me another ten shillings, but it cost more to stay there and to spend my time visiting London. With my loan deducted at source, my first monthly cheque came to only eleven pounds. There was little to spare for clothes and entertainment. Fortunately Woolworths was literally a sixpenny store in those days; silk stockings were a constant necessity and cost sixpence each leg. Mother still made clothes for me, providing at least a new suit each spring and autumn.

After a while Amy Lee from Bristol, the art teacher, and I moved into digs together. This was more congenial. We could exchange ideas, share our entertaining, and we both had an insatiable appetite for new books, which we swapped and discussed. There were so many new young writers in the Thirties; we absorbed Vera Brittain, Winifred Holtby, Dorothy L. Sayers,

Back home at Woodville and taking it easy in the garden.

Aldous Huxley; in particular I loved Rosamund Lehmann. We read aloud to each other the purple passages from *Cold Comfort Farm*, and tried to do the *New Statesman* puzzles. We were discouraged in the face of Allan M. Laing's brilliance.

They were gay and heady times, lived against an international backcloth which constantly jerked us back to reality. Rumours of concentration camps reached us as we watched Hitler's rise to power. We talked peace, ran our LNU groups, and invited informed people to talk to the children, but we were not so politically aware as the present generation. We had no television and not every home had a radio; we relied on a responsible press. So much of the time we pushed it all behind us and enjoyed our freedom.

The girls' school made up two sides of a quadrangle; a boys' school flanked the other two sides. Since we were new schools, almost all the staff on both sides were young and unmarried. There were dances and theatre parties; and school plays to produce on a beautifully equipped stage with grey velvet curtains, a collection of blocks for abstract stage settings, and, for me the most lavish of all, banks of lights with dimmers. I was proud to produce two school plays: Beaumont and Fletcher's *Knight of the Burning Pestle* and, more ambitiously, with Grace Earnshaw, the music teacher, Masefield's *Coming of Christ*. I was quite inexperienced and dependent on one of the men's staff to work out a lighting plan with me and build the sets. Rehearsing the large casts was daunting enough.

There were then no such things as posts of special responsibility, commanding extra salaries, so there was no rapid turnover of staff searching for betterment. We worked very hard, and with my subjects I was always coping with vast piles of marking.

The children were fun and I enjoyed teaching. I suspect they were enthusiastic because I was young and they never knew what I was going to get up to next. I was happy to turn the classroom into a stage at the drop of a hat or to sit on the floor and tell stories; and not every teacher has to stand on a chair to reach the top half of the blackboard. I admire teachers who are dedicated to remedial work, or who teach infants. I should have been hopeless; I was not peaceful enough or slow enough. I needed children to stimulate me as I tried to stimulate them. Infants would have created bedlam.

At every stage in my life I have been lucky to meet someone special who has influenced me greatly, and introduced me to new pastures. Miss Stewart, the headmistress, was one of these; a very special person, highly sensitive and sympathetic, interested in the arts and passionately devoted to justice and human rights. She resembled Virginia Woolf, with the same long finely-chiselled face

120

and sad haunting eyes. She felt a strange affinity with Virginia Woolf, too. It was she who lent me *A Room of One's Own* and *Three Guineas*. Her choice of paintings in the classrooms included many reproductions of Gauguin's Tahitian period. There was a smouldering passion in her, sometimes surfacing to scorn the insensitivity of male colleagues and sometimes erupting in an indignant storming at a class which had badly misbehaved. Usually she spoke with a quiet voice, listening sympathetically to troubles, expecting a high standard of everyone and commenting on events with a wry sense of humour. She hated phoniness and injustice, and suffered for every ill-treated group of prisoners of conscience in any country. She was lit with an inner spirit. The men found her difficult to work with; I found her inspiring, and the children loved and respected her, while treading warily in her presence.

Richard Church came down to judge one of our poetry festivals. He obviously sensed her special qualities, and afterwards inquired of me, "How do the children feel about her?" I suspect she made men feel uncomfortable.

I occasionally took older members of my school LNU branch to London to hear speakers like Vernon Bartlett and Noel Baker. At

The home of the Davidsson family at Saltsjöbaden, Stockholm.

one meeting a master and several boys from Mill Hill enthused on an exchange system they had built up with a Swedish school, and recommended it to us. I inquired if I could avail myself of it, and I was put in touch with Miss Areskög, a teacher of English in Saltsjöbaden, who found a family to welcome me. This was my first holiday abroad; Father saw me off at Tilbury on the Swedish-Lloyd line, a little apprehensive as he waved goodbye. The inevitable trunk came too.

I fell in love with Sweden. I stayed with a delightful family, the Davidssons, with two daughters, the eldest eighteen; we have remained friends ever since. We lived in a large modern bungalow among pine woods at Saltsjöbaden, with blueberries covering the ground, a variety of edible toadstools, and everywhere the scent of pines. I marvelled at the careless use of the telephone; apparently it was so cheap that it was unnecessary to run next door with a message, they always picked up the phone. They showed me Stockholm, only a few miles away, lovely on its numerous islands, clean and affluent, where shops sold goods of high quality which seemed to have escaped the bad design proliferating in England as

I am on the left, with Gullan Davidsson and her two daughters, Gunvor and Britta, in Stockholm.

Father, Mother and "G" in the gardens at Woodville, Matching Tye.

factories churned out mass-produced monstrosities. Lampshades, I remember, were particular atrocities in England then; in Sweden they were pleasing.

I learnt not to sip wine at dinner until I had been "skol"ed by my host, and not to greet strangers until I had been introduced. I was amazed to see the girls curtsey to their elders, even when meeting them casually in the street, and to their mother when they thanked her formally for each meal. It was a courteous, uncluttered world.

The Davidssons took me to Skansen, the outdoor museum outside Stockholm, to the Opera to hear Jussi Börling singing in *La Bohème*, to Drottingholm with its royal theatre, and on a boating weekend to Sandham, the furthermost point in the Stockholm archipelago. It was a new and enchanting way of life. I was not to return to Sweden until after the war with my husband and three of my young children, but the Swedes visited us in England. Britta came the following year to stay with me, and after the war returned to take a post-graduate degree at Newnham.

Then came 1937, a wonderful year. A new member had joined the staff of the boys' school, young and handsome and full of energy. We had fallen in love, and found each other absorbing. We became engaged, my mother insisting he be called "G" because

123

Ruth had recently married a George, and she was not going to have two sons-in-law with the same name.

G and I spent as much time as we could together. He was born in London and went to Bancroft's School, Woodford Green, but he became as passionately fond of the country as I was. He came often to Matching with me, walking miles every weekend, often in pouring rain, which we hardly noticed. There was so much to talk about and to discover about each other. My mother despaired of us ever getting up from the breakfast table.

We watched with mixed feelings the appeasement policy of Neville Chamberlain and the resulting Munich agreement: we hoped it would work, but were ashamed of the sell-out of Czechoslovakia. Together we organised a Peace Exhibition in Chingford in conjunction with all the other peace movements— perhaps to salve our consciences.

We were married at Matching church in 1939 at the beginning of August, and returned from our honeymoon blissfully happy and irresponsibly oblivious of anything but ourselves. We were shocked to find our friends so anxious about the news from Europe, and so certain that war was imminent.

A new term was due to begin, so we met at school on Sunday, 3rd September, for a Staff meeting. One of the men had brought his radio with him.

We gathered in his room to hear Neville Chamberlain's ominous announcement that Britain was at war. No-one spoke. Miss Stewart stood with the tears running down her cheeks. Three couples were newly married; none of us had any idea of what was in store for us.

For the next six years war dominated our lives. Three of our four children were born in this period. They would find it part of theirs. Perhaps it would not be such an infinitesimal part as the First World War had been of my life, over twenty years before.

Index

Illustrations in **bold** *type*

A
Agra, 88
Alcott, Louisa M., 8, 95
Allan, M. M., 106–107
Anderson, David, 31
Anti-War Society, Cambridge, 111
Army and Navy Stores, 16
Aunt Lizzie, 39–40
Aunt Tilly, 66

B
Baden-Powell, Lord, 51
Baird, Phyllis, 26
Balfour, Mr, 1, 62
Barker's, 16
Benares, 87
Bertha, 48–49
Billericay, 101
Birdie, 57
Bishop's Stortford, 42, 50, 67, 74, 77,
    83, 89–92, 98
Blackberries, 11
Blacksmith, 69–70
Blenheim Oranges, 9
Boathouse, **20**
Boer War, 81
Booth, Dr Norman, 67
Boy Scouts, Matching, 52
    Suffolk, 37
Braintree, 42
Bridge of Sighs, **116**
Brinkworth, Dora, **58**, 98
    Reverend J. B., 4, 56, 117
Broom Hills, Stoke, 48
Buckhurst Hill, 4
Bury St Edmunds, 54
Bye, bye, blackbird, 50
Byford family, 78

C
Cab, 33
Cadogan, Earl of, 54
Calverley, Mrs, 51, 52, 56
Cambridge, 17, 34, 99, 107–115
    High School for Girls, 115
Carey, Rosa Nouchette, 95
Chapel, Matching Tye, 59–63, 68, 74
    Stoke-by-Nayland, 36–37
Cherrytree Farm, Polstead, 47–48
Chingford, 119
Christmas, 3, 4, 9, 63

Churchgate School, Harlow, 23–26,
    23, 55
Churchman, Miss, 15–16
Church, Richard, 121
Colchester, 42, 44
Coleman, Miss, 26
Co-optimists, 1
Commons Lane, Matching, 61
Corder, William, 47–48
Coronation of George VI, 54
Council houses, 8, 75, 76
Cousin George, 80–81
Cousins, Mr, 107
Cox's Orange Pippins, 9
Crabbe, Mr and Mrs, 3, 16, 22–23
Cromwell, Oliver, 79
Crowe, Mr, 57
Cutforth, Sir Arthur, 114

D
Dalton's Farm, Stoke-by-Nayland, 85
Dances, 63
Davidsson family, 122, **122**
Day, Dr Tom, 67
    Dr Newcombe, 67
Delhi Durbar, 88
Digby Road, London, 79
Doodlebugs, 4
Dovercourt Bay, 106
Downs, The, Stoke-by-Nayland, 34–36
Down Hall, Matching, 18–19, 51, **52**,
    56–57
D'Oyly Carte Opera Company, 114
Drottingholm, Sweden, 123
Dummy, 18

E
Easter, 62–63
Edwards, millers, 77
Edwards, Mr F. C., 77
Epping, 33, 70
    St Margarets, 49
Essex County Council,
    Education Committee, 100
    Library Service, 95
Essex Hunt, 10, 51, 75
Essex Point-to-point, 75-77

F
Faggoters, Matching, 103, **103**
Farthing, Mrs, 22

Fens, The, 17
Fenton family, 59, 60, **71**, 72, 76
Festival Theatre, 114
Fletcher, Emily, 5, **32**, 33–37, **35**, 42,
  105
  Robert, 33–37, **35**, 85
Ford cars, 72
Fox, The, Matching Tye, 66

G
"G", 123–24, **123**
Games, 21, 27
Garden House Hotel, Cambridge, 113
General Strike, The, 90–91
Gibbins family, 21
Gielgud, John, 97
Gipsies, 70–71
Girl Guides, Matching, 52–54, **53**
Girton College, Cambridge, 100, 101,
  107
Glennie, Miss, 115
Goodnight Sweetheart, 107
Grantchester, 114, 117
Great War, The, 1, 3, 16–17, 21, 33,
  58, 81
Guiness, Hon. Mrs Ernest, 113
Guthrie, Tyrone, 114

H
Hadleigh, 44
Hall, Henry, 98
Hammill, Miss, 90, 97, 99–100
Harding-Jones, Frank, 7, 102
  Gladys, 52–54
  Henry, 100
  Phyllis, 52–54
Hare and Hounds, Matching Tye, **14**,
  16, 66
Harlow, 1, 14, 21, 30, 33, 55, 67, 70,
  73, 78, 89
Harlow College, 71, **72**, 101
Harper, Mrs, 56
Harrods, 16
Harsley, Nurse, 68
Harvest, 28–30
Hatfield Heath, 91
Hawkins, Mr and Mrs, 73
  Hilda, 74
Haymaking, 27–28
Haymeads, Bishop's Stortford, 49–50
Heath and Heather's herb tobacco, 72
Helpman, Robert, 98
Herts and Essex High School, 26, 89,
  90, 93, 95–100, **99**
High Laver, 20, 103
Hockley family, 78

Holborn, 81
Homerton College, 99, 106–109, **108,**
  109
Housham Hall, Matching, 19, 73
Housham Tye, 7
Howard, Mr and Mrs John, 57, 58, 65
  Mr and Mrs Tom, 77
Huntingdon, 17
  Old Grammar School, 79, 81

I
Il Traumerei, 38
India, 1, 85–88, **84, 86, 88**
Infant Welfare Clinic, 9, 68
Inge, Dean, 113
Iphigenia in Aulis, 113
Italian Art Exhibition, Royal
  Academy, 97

J
Jazz, 98, 113

K
Kilmory Castle, 53
King's College Chapel, **112,** 117
Kingstons, Matching, 77

L
Laing, Allan M., 120
Lamplighter, The, 8
Laurels, The, Stoke-by-Nayland, **40,**
  105
Lawrence, Dr, 117
League of Nations, 97, 111
Letters from the Front, 1
Lewis, Miss Gaynor, 96–97
Lily Pond, 17–20, **18**, 58
Little, Mrs, 21, **22**
Locke, John, 20
Lord, Mr and Mrs, 44, 48
  Dick, 44
Loughton, 33
Lucknow, 87
Luttman, Mrs, 86

M
Man Wood, Matching, 75
Marten, Maria, 47
Marriage Feast Room, Matching, 55
Masham, Lady, 20
Matching Tye, 1–16, 65–66, 69
  Church, **5,** 55–58, **57,** 121
  Green, 26, 59, 65, 69, 72, 75, 104
  Hall, 19, 55, 57, 65
  Vicarage, 3, 16, 55, 98
  Wood, 1, 10–11, 75

Maples, 8
May Day, 110
Men's Club, 78
Moor Hall, 1, 22, 62
Moorhens, 17, 19
Mulberry Green, 67
Murray, Professor Gilbert, 113
Muscovy ducks, 19
Music, 98
Music Hall songs, 80, 81

N
Nelson, Publishers, 62
Newman's End, Matching, 21
Newport Grammar School, 93
North Weald, *The Talbot*, 103
North-West Frontier, India, 81, 88
Nottage, Miss, 21

O
Oates Barn, 20
  Hall, 20
Oates, Titus, 20
Odham's Press, 103
Oil stoves, 7, 8, 61
Orchard, Woodville, 5, 9–10, **11**
Oxford Group, 113

P
Paraffin, 4, 7, 61
Parish, Dorothy, 59
Park Road, Stoke-by-Nayland, 44
Payne, Jack, 98
Peacock family, 78
Pea-picking, 69–70
Peartree, Mrs, 37–38
Peggles, 56
Polstead, 37, 38, 46–49, **49**
  "Blacks", 47
  Red Barn, 47–48
Ponds, 17–19
Poona, 87
Porter, Sir Leslie and Lady, 86
Post Office, Matching Tye, 13
  Matching Green, 72
Potters Bar, 3
Potter Street, 62, 70, 103
Princess Mary, 54
Privies, 8
Pumps, Matching Tye, 4, 13
  Matching School, 5

R
Read, Miss, 117
Red Cross, 3
Retreat, The, Theydon Bois, 33

Ribston Pippins, 9
Riddlestone, Charlie, 37, 85
  Lizzie, 37, 85
Roadmender, 3, 23
Roothings (Rodings), 72
Round House, Matching, 65
Rowley, Sir Joshua and Lady, 85
Royal Horse Artillery, 1, 81
Rye Street Hospital, Bishop's Stort-
  ford, 67

S
St John's College, Cambridge, 34,
  111, 112, **112**, 117
St Petersburg, 16
Salmon, Henry, 79–81, **80**
  Kate, 1–5, 8–11, 30, 33, 55–58, 61,
    72, **82**, **84**, **86**, **104**
  Louisa, 79–81, **80**, **82**
  Ruth, 1–6, 15, 16, 21–24, 33, 37–48,
    50–57, 62, 71–78, **82**, 83, 87, **91**,
    93, 98, 101, **102**
  Walter, 1–5, **2**, 8–11, **25**, 30, 33,
    55–58, 60, 72, **82**, **84**, **86**, **104**
Saville, Mr, 69–70
  Horace, 69–70
Sawbridgeworth, 13, 114
Sawdy, Mr, 37
School Attendance Officer, 25
Scotland Street, Stoke-by-Nayland,
  36, **45**
Scott, Mr, 62, 70
Scudamore's boathouse, 114
Second World War, 3, 4, 44, 87, 123
Seymour family, 78
Seymour, Mrs, 92
Sheering, 51, 91, 93
Shetlocks Farm, Matching, **28**, 71–72
Sir Roger de Coverley, 63
Silcocks, 72
Skansen, 123
Smith, Mr, 13–15, 59
Sports day, 54
Steam-ploughs, 30
Stephens, Bessie, 72–73
  Sam, 72–73
Stewart, Miss, 120
Stock Hall, Matching, 72–73
Stoke-by-Nayland, 33–45, 50
  Flower Show, 50
Suffolk, 5, 33–49
  Punch, 27
Sundays, 8, 55, 59
Sunday School, 1, 34
Sunlight Soap, 8
Sweden, 122–123

T
Taj Mahal, 88
Tendring Hall, Stoke-by-Nayland, 50,
  85
Tennyson, Alfred Lord, 95–96
Thaxted, 101
The Prime of Miss Jean Brodie, 90
There is a green hill, 9
Theydon Bois, 33
Thorpe-le-Soken, 53
Threshing machines, 30
Tinney, Edgar, 74
  John, 74
Tiptree, 101
Tramps, 48–50
Trevelyan, Professor G. M., 114
Triennial Mission, Cambridge, 112
Tricycle, 60

U
Uncle Tom's Cabin, 8

V
Valley Farm, 37, **43**, 44
Veleta, 63
Vicarage, Matching, 3, 4, 16, 55, 98
Village school, 5, 21
Village shop, **12**, 13
Virgil, 80

W
Walls, Mr and Mrs, 59–61, **60**, **61**, 94
Wantz Lane, Matching, 61
Waring and Gillow, 16
Wash-house, 5, 8–9
Water supply, 4, 5, 7
Waterhouse, Dr, 109, 117
Webber, Mr and Mrs, 23–26
Welham, Emmie, **38**, 39, 41–43, 50,
  105
  Frank and Mary-Ann, 36, 40–43,
  105
Well Field, 43, 50
Whitbread family, 78
Whiteley's, 16
Wicks, Miss, 51, 56–57
Wilkinson, Reverend Horace, 85, 86
Wilton, Lord, 114
Women's Institute, 21, 51, 62, 63, 78,
  98
Women's Meeting, 9
Woodford Green, 4
Wood, Mrs Henry, 8
Woodville, Matching, 6–11, **6**, **10**, **11**,
  66, 71, 72, 83, 92, **118**
Woolf, Virginia, 121

Z
Zeppelin, 3